6 YEAR

Classworks
Literacy

Paula Ross

Acknowledgements

The author and publishers wish to thank the following for permission to use copyright material:

Street Child © Berlie Doherty. Reprinted by permission of HarperCollins Publishers Ltd.

Queen Victoria © 1998 Stacie Farley, *The World of Royalty*, **http://www.royalty.nu**

Pipe Dreams © Kit Wright, included by permission of the author.

Judy Blume – the official bio, by permission of the author, **http://www.judyblume.com**

Isambard Kingdon Brunel © 2003 David Ross and Britain Express, **http://www.britainexpress.com**

David Beckham Portrait of a Superstar by Fergus Kelly text © Fergus Kelly, 2001. All rights reserved. Reproduced by permission of Scholastic Ltd.

'The Mirror' from *Collected Poems* by Sylvia Plath, reprinted by permission of Faber & Faber Ltd.

Roger Butts for 'Poem in the shape of the causeway leading to St Michael's Mount, which appears at low tide'.

Gina Douthwaite for 'Night Mer'.

Faber and Faber Ltd for Philip Gross, 'Daughter of the Sea' from *All Nite Cafe* by Philip Gross; and Ted Hughes, 'My Granny' from *Meet My Folks* by Ted Hughes (1961).

David Higham Associates on behalf of the author for Charles Causley, 'Morwenstow' from *Jack the Treacle Eater* by Charles Causley, Macmillan; and Charles Causley, 'How the Sea' from *The Young Man of Cury and Other Poems* by Charles Causley, Macmillan.

Parents Information Network for material from their web page on 'Texting', www. pin.org.uk/safety/safetyset.htm.

The Society of Authors as the Literary Representative of the Estate of the Author for John Masefield, 'A Wanderer's Song' and 'Sea-Fever'.

Road Safety Leaflet reproduced with the permission of Cornwall County Council, Road Safety Unit.

'Fog' from *Chicago Poems* by Carl Sandburg, copyright 1916 by Holt, Rinehart and Winston and renewed 1944 by Carl Sandburg, reprinted by permission of Harcourt, Inc.

Cover photo by Chad Baker/Ryan McVay/Getty Images.

Contents

Unit	Outcome	Objectives	Page
Journalistic Writing	A newspaper article based on a well-known story using ICT	S1 T8, T12, T15, T16, T18	1
Long-established Poets	A poem that shows experimentation with active verbs and personification, both written and performed	S1 T3, T5, T10	11
Autobiography and Diaries	Extract from an autobiography of a fictional character linked to history topic 'What was it like for children living in Victorian Britain?' (QCA Unit 11)	S4, S6 T11, T14, T17	23
Biographical Writing	Biography of a mountaineer, using ICT (cross-curricular link to QCA Unit 15 'The Mountain Environment')	S2, S3, S5 T11, T14, T17, T18	37
Classic Fiction: *Treasure Island*	A summary of R.L. Stevenson's text in a specified number of words; an extract with two narrators; a narration of a modern version of a quest story; an extract written in the style and voice of the text; a playscript of an extract	S1, S4, S5, S6 T2, T3, T4, T5, T6, T7, T8, T9	51
Non-chronological Reports	Information leaflets on mountain ranges, including comparative reports (cross-curricular link to QCA topic 'Mountains')	S1, S4, S5 T12, T13, T17, T18	104
Discussion	A written discussion paper and a class debate	S3, S5 T15, T16, T18, T19	121
Formal Writing	A leaflet giving safety guidance about children's use of technology; a formal letter to headteachers about the leaflet	S2, S3, S4 T17, T20	138
Non-fiction Texts: Explanation	Revision of Science AT4 'Physical Processes – The Earth and Beyond', and aspects of AT3	S1, S3 T15, T16	160
Poetry on a Theme: 'The Sea'	A class anthology on the theme of 'The Sea'	S2 T2, T3, T4, T7, T12, T13	177

Introduction

How Classworks works

What this book contains

- Chunks of text, both annotated and 'blank' for your own annotations.

- Checklists (or toolkits), planning frames, storyboards, scaffolds and other writing aids.

- Examples of modelled, supported and demonstration writing.

- Lesson ideas including key questions and plenary support.

- Marking ladders for structured self-assessment.

- Blocked unit planning with suggested texts, objectives and outcomes.

- Word-level starter ideas to complement the daily teaching of phonics, handwriting and other skills.

- There are no scripts, no worksheets and nothing you can't change to suit your needs.

How this book is organised

- There are blocked units of work (see previous page) lasting between one week and several, depending on the text type.

- Each blocked unit is organised into a series of chunks of teaching content.

- Each 'chunk' has accompanying checklists and other photocopiable resources.

- For every text we *suggest* annotations, checklists and marking ladders.

- Every unit follows the *teaching sequence for writing* found in *Grammar for Writing* (DfES, 2000).

- You can mix and match teaching ideas, units and checklists as you see fit.

How you can use *Classworks* with your medium-term plan

- Refer to your medium-term planning for the blocking of NLS objectives.

- Find the text-type you want to teach (or just the objectives).

- Use the contents page to locate the relevant unit.

- Familiarise yourself with the text and language features using *Classworks* checklists and exemplar analysis pages, and DfES or QCA resources such as *Grammar for Writing*.

- Browse the lesson ideas and photocopiables to find what you want to use.

- You can just use the text pages … photocopy and adapt the checklists … use or change some of the teaching ideas … take whatever you want and adapt it to fit your class.

Planning a blocked unit of work with Classworks

Classworks units exemplify a blocked unit approach to planning the teaching of Literacy. What follows is an outline of this method of planning and teaching, and how *Classworks* can help you

You need: *Classworks* Literacy Year 6, medium-term planning; OHT (optional).
Optional resources: your own choice of texts for extra analysis; *Grammar for Writing*.

Method

- From the medium-term planning, identify the **outcome**, **texts** and **objectives** you want to teach.

- *Classworks* units **exemplify** how some units could be planned, resourced and taught.

- Decide how to 'chunk' the text you are analysing, for example, introductory paragraph, paragraph 1, paragraph 2, closing paragraph.

- *Classworks* units give an example of **chunking** with accompanying resources and exemplar analysis. Texts for pupil analysis (labelled 'Pupil copymaster') are intended for whole class display on an OHT.

- **Whatever you think of the checklists provided, analyse the text with *your* class and build *your own* checklist for the whole text, and for each chunk.**

- Plan your blocked unit based on the following teaching sequence for writing.

- *Classworks* units outline one way of planning a **blocked unit**, with exemplifications of some days, and suggestions for teaching content on others.

Shared Reading – analysing the text – create 'checklist' or writer's toolkit	The children analyse another of that text type and add to checklist	Review checklist
Shared Writing – demonstrate application of 'checklist' to a small piece of writing	The children write independently based on your demonstration	Use examples on OHT to check against the 'checklist'

- This model is only a guideline, allowing the writing process to be scaffolded. You would want to build in opportunities for planning for writing, talking for writing, teaching explicit word-level and sentence-level objectives that would then be modelled in the shared writing, and so on. There are ideas for word-level and sentence-level starters on pages 197–200.

- Allow opportunities for the children to be familiar with the text type. This might include reading plenty of examples, drama, role play, video, and so on.

Assessment

- Make sure that 'checklists' are displayed around the room and referred to before writing and when assessing writing in the **plenary**.

- One or two children could work on an OHT, which could be the focus of the plenary.

- Use a **marking ladder** for the children to evaluate their writing. This is based on the checklist your class has built up. We give you an example of how it might look for each blocked unit. There's a blank copy on page 201.

What each page does

Text-type written large at the top, and then on every page.

What a unit based on this material might look like.

Shaded sections refer to *Classworks* ideas, white sections to suggested extra content.

Text-based outcome clearly signalled.

Objectives spelt out.

Key aspects of teaching this text type listed.

Child-friendly outcomes for every chunk of content.

Clear headings for each section of the page.

Main idea broken up into bullets and key questions.

Board-work examples highlighted clearly.

***Classworks* resources referenced wherever relevant.**

Brief independent, pair or guided work idea.

Plenary guidance.

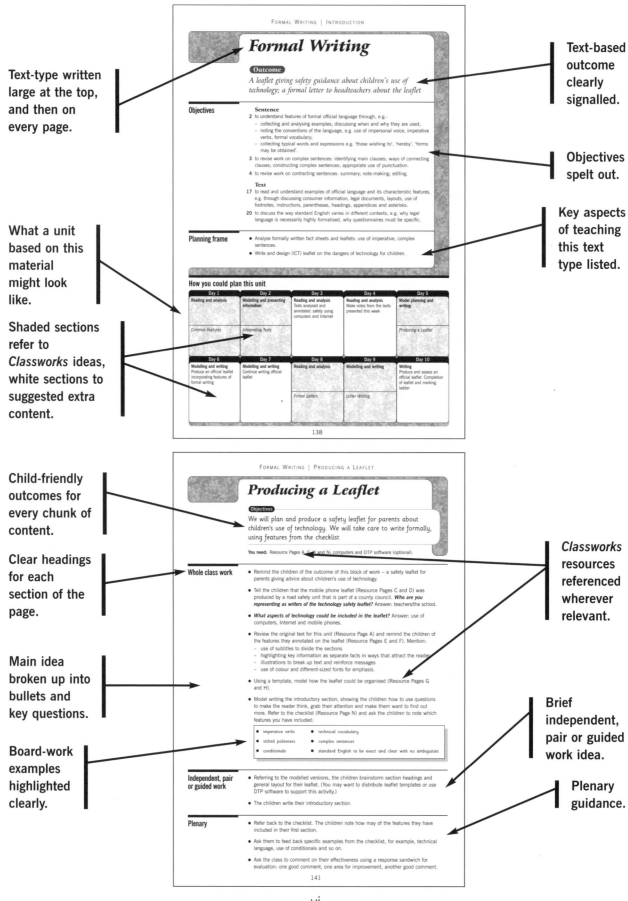

Journalistic Writing

Outcome

A newspaper article based on a well-known story using ICT

Objectives

Sentence

1 to revise from Yr 5 the different word classes.

Text

8 to summarise a passage, chapter or text in a specified number of words.

12 to comment critically on the language, style, success of examples of non-fiction.

15 to develop a journalistic style through considering:
- the interest of the reader
- selection and presentation of information.

16 to use the styles and conventions of journalism to report on, e.g. real or imagined events.

18 to use IT to plan, revise, edit writing to improve accuracy and conciseness and to bring it to publication standard.

Planning frame

- Read and analyse text features of newspaper articles.

- Use these text features to write a newspaper article, including: headlines, opening paragraphs, quotes, least important information first.

How you could plan this unit

Day 1	Day 2	Day 3	Day 4	Day 5
Reading	Writing	Reading Analysis of bias	Writing Planning	Reading
Analysing Articles	*Headlines*			*Opening Sentences*

Day 6	Day 7	Day 8	Day 9	Day 10
Writing	Writing Middle paragraphs	Writing Final paragraphs	Reading Editing	Writing Checklists and marking ladder
Opening Paragraphs				

Analysing Articles

Objective

We will read newspaper articles and analyse them to discover the language and style used

You need: Resource Pages A, B and D; OHT or photocopy of an article from local or national paper; selection of local newspapers for paired work.

Whole class work

- View OHT of chosen article with your class. Read the article aloud and discuss.

- *Is the content clear? Is it interesting?*

- *What is the viewpoint of the writer?* Point out that the writer is not always a journalist – the article may be an opinion piece. *Is the article objective or does it express the writer's opinion?*

- Use an OHT of Resource Page A, and refer to Resource Page B, to model analysing an article.

- In pairs, the children read and share their thoughts on the style and structure of the text.

- As a whole class, the children offer their ideas – these are used to start to build a class checklist (see checklist 1, Resource Page D for ideas.) Ensure that the discussion covers headlines, opening sentence and structure of the story.

- Explain that newspaper articles are planned as an inverted triangle ▼ – most important information first, least important last. First paragraphs should be full of detail. This is because the sub-editor will cut stories working from the final paragraph up if they need space.

Independent, pair or guided work

- Distribute pages of local newspapers. Ask the children to highlight and annotate features noted in the shared reading. *Is there consistency?*

Plenary

- Ask the children to go to a designated corner of the classroom, depending on whether they know two, three, four or more than four conventions of journalistic writing.

- Each child tells the rest of their group which features they know. If by doing this they hear about other features, the children should move on to the relevant corner and repeat the task.

- Take feedback from the groups in each corner.

- Add any other noted features to the checklist. This should be displayed throughout the teaching of this unit.

Headlines

Objective

We will be writing headlines from well-known stories, in newspaper headline format

You need: Resource Page D; software with a newspaper-format template (or a paper copy); word processor; display paper; articles from previous lesson.

Whole class work

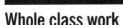

- Copy some headlines from articles examined in previous lessons on to the board.

- Discuss the function of headlines and how effective they are in these cases. ***Do they give a good idea of the story? Do they hook you into wanting to read on?***

- Focus on the words used:
  - short words
  - omission of words, especially verbs and articles
  - use of wordplay.

- Write on the board:

CIRCUS	DEATH	SHOCK

- Identify the use of nouns as adjectives. Start to make a class checklist for headlines (see checklist 2, Resource Page D for ideas). ***Newspapers love to use wordplay in headlines. Why do you think this is? When is it appropriate/not appropriate?***

- Model rewriting some headlines in longer format, noting aloud the changes you make. ***Why doesn't it work?***

- Using a word processor (or paper), model possible headlines for *The Three Little Pigs* (example 4, Resource Page D). Refer to the class checklist as you do so.

- Using newspaper template software, choose the most suitable font and text size.

- Decide with the class which one of your modelled headlines is most effective and why, and cut and paste it into the newspaper template.

Independent, pair or guided work

- Each pair of children selects a well-known story, myth, legend or fairy tale.

- The children who need extra support should use the story modelled in the unit.

- The children open and save a copy of the newspaper template and a word-processing document. Together, they brainstorm and word-process a number of possible headlines.

- The children decide which is the most effective and cut and paste into their saved newspaper template.

Plenary

- Each pair of children prints out (or writes) a headline from their brainstorm and displays it on the board.

- As a class, order the headlines from the most successful to least successful. Discuss why some are more successful than others.

- Add any relevant points to the class checklist for headlines and display the poster.

Opening Sentences

Objective

We will analyse and list the key points covered in a newspaper story's opening paragraph

You need: Resource Pages C and D; articles from previous lessons; strips of paper for copying sentences; large sheet of paper for checklist.

Whole class work

- With your class, read together a number of opening sentences, followed by the whole of a first paragraph.

- Ask the children to identify the style and structure of the sentences. For example, see if opening paragraphs:

> give key facts
>
> are densely packed with information
>
> have the first sentence as whole paragraph (in many cases)

- Introduce the idea that the first paragraph must *count* and may be the only paragraph read, so it should:

> carry a strong image and rivet the reader's attention
>
> be clear, direct and personal, using active verbs
>
> answer the questions who, what, when, where, why

- Count how many words there are typically in a first paragraph.

Independent, pair or guided work

- Ask the children to examine the opening sentences/paragraphs from selected articles. Using Resource Page C as an example, the children record answers to who, what, when, where and why questions for selected texts.

Plenary

- Ask the children to contribute ideas to a class checklist for first sentences of newspaper articles (see checklist 3, Resource Page D for ideas). Display the checklist in the classroom throughout this unit.

Opening Paragraphs

Objective

We will write an opening paragraph for an article using our checklist

You need: Resource Page D; software offering a newspaper format template (or paper copy).

Whole class work

- With your class, review the information included on the checklist for opening sentences. Note how many words there were in opening paragraphs.

- Ask the children what information needs to go into the opening paragraph of the story of *The Three Little Pigs*. Write their suggestions on the board. For example:

  > wolf blows down two houses
  >
  > pigs then seek shelter with their brother
  >
  > wolf is killed

- Model turning this information into an opening paragraph within the word limit (see example 5, Resource Page D).

- *Does the paragraph answer the who, what, when, where, why and how questions?*

Independent, pair or guided work

- Individually or in pairs, ask the children to write their own first paragraphs using the checklist.

- Some children will need additional support. Underline a number of words in the modelled paragraph and ask them to use a thesaurus to change the words.

- Other children could experiment with changing the order of the clauses in their sentence(s) to see which reads the most fluently.

Plenary

- Ask the children to pass their first paragraph to another pair of children. Ask them to assess: *Does the paragraph answer the who, what, when, where, why questions? Does it fulfil the requirements identified on the checklist for first sentences?*

- Encourage different pairs to feed back to each other.

- Display one or two good examples next to your class checklist.

5

What features of journalistic writing can you recognise here?

VAN DRIVER HITS CYCLIST

THE DRIVER of a van that struck a 64-year-old cyclist taking part in his 12th Land's End to John O'Groats run, had been retrieving a folder from the floor just beforehand, Truro court heard this week.

Benjamin Nathan Walters, aged 30 of Elm Road, Teignmouth, pleaded guilty to driving without due care and attention and was fined £500 and banned from driving for four months.

Mr Stephens, the cyclist, suffered injuries to his back and shoulder. He was taken by air ambulance to Truro hospital.

Irene Parnell, prosecuting, said, "Mr Stephens was hit from behind, propelled into a hedge, and landed face down." A number of witnesses had seen the van suddenly veer to the nearside and collide with Mr Stephens, who was not wearing a cycle helmet but had on a bright yellow reflective jacket.

Brian Shore, a friend, said it had been one of those awful accidents. Ben Walters was a good driver and had not been speeding and had never been involved in an accident before.

He worked as a driver, delivering mail order catalogues and for the past 10 years had driven 50,000 miles a year.

(Exemplar analysis)

Example of analysis of journalistic writing

Headline to attract reader's attention.

VAN DRIVER HITS CYCLIST

THE DRIVER of a van that struck a 64 year old cyclist taking part in his 12th Land's End to John O'Groats run, had been retrieving a folder from the floor just beforehand, Truro court heard this week.

Benjamin Nathan Walters, aged 30 of Elm Road, Teignmouth, pleaded guilty to driving without due care and attention and was fined £500 and banned from driving for four months.

Mr Stephens, the cyclist, suffered injuries to his back and shoulder. He was taken by air ambulance to Truro hospital.

Irene Parnell, prosecuting, said, "Mr Stephens was hit from behind, propelled into a hedge, and landed face down." A number of witnesses had seen the van suddenly veer to the nearside and collide with Mr Stephens, who was not wearing a cycle helmet but had on a bright yellow reflective jacket.

Brian Shore, a friend, said it had been one of those awful accidents. Ben Walters was a good driver and had not been speeding and had never been involved in an accident before.

He worked as a driver, delivering mail order catalogues and for the past 10 years had driven 50,000 miles a year.

First paragraph summarises the whole article.

Further paragraphs becoming increasingly less important to the story.

Quote.

Article includes opinions and facts.

First paragraph answers questions – who, what, where, when, why.

Viewpoints given from others who witnessed the event.

Final paragraph least important so could be cut if sub-editors need more space for other stories.

Who, what, where, when, why?

STUDENT of the year at Camborne Pool Redruth College beauty faculty is Lynette French, of Hayle, who works at the Lion Hotel, Camborne. She was presented with the award by college principal Harry Wilkinson at the faculty's annual prizegiving in the Drama Studio, on Tuesday.

Who? *Lynette French*

Where? *Drama Studio at the college*

When? *Last Tuesday*

What? *Presentation of award*

Why? *For being the best student*

(Exemplar material)

Checklists and models for journalistic writing

Example of a checklist for journalistic writing ①

- Use headlines
- Quote from different people connected to the story
- Write the first word in CAPITALS
- Article answers who, what, when, where, why questions
- Include different people's points of view
- Include facts

Example of a checklist for writing headlines ②

- Use bold letters
- Use powerful words
- Make sure it attracts attention
- Make it short and punchy
- Phrases not sentences
- Use CAPITAL letters
- Make sure it makes the article more serious, exciting, funny, and so on
- Use word play
- Determiners are often missing

Example of a checklist for writing first sentences ③

- Make sure it is jam-packed with information
- Tell the main points of the story
- Try to get the reader to read on
- The first sentence is often the entire first paragraph

Model headlines for *The Three Little Pigs* ④

WOLF MAKES PIGS HOMELESS

PIGS SHELTER AS WOLF DEVASTATES HOMES

WOLF FINDS SURPRISE IN CHIMNEY

PIGS TAKE TO THEIR TROTTERS

WOLF PUFFED OUT

Model of a first paragraph for *The Three Little Pigs* ⑤

A WOLF, who had been in hot pursuit of three little pigs, was killed when he fell down a chimney in Phil Pig's house, into a cauldron of scalding water, on Friday 13th April. The wolf had earlier blown down the cottages of Percy and Paula Pig who had gone on to seek shelter with their brother, Phil.

Classworks Literacy Year 6 © Paula Ross, Nelson Thornes Ltd 2003

Marking ladder

Name: _____

Pupil	Objective	Teacher
	My article has a short effective headline.	
	My first paragraph is packed with information.	
	It provides a strong image and hooks the reader.	
	The beginning of my article answers the questions who, what, where, when, why?	
	My article is organised into many paragraphs.	
	I have included quotes from both sides.	
	I have based it on an inverted triangle: as the article progresses, the details become less important.	
	What could I do to improve my article next time?	

Long-established Poets

Outcome

A poem that shows experimentation with active verbs and personification, both written and performed

Objectives

Sentence

1 to revise from Y5 the different word classes.

Text

3 to articulate personal responses to literature, identifying why and how a text affects the reader.

5 to contribute constructively to shared discussion about literature, responding to and building on the views of others.

10 to write own poems experimenting with active verbs and personification; produce revised poems for reading aloud individually.

Planning frame

- Read and analyse personification and active verbs in poems by long-established authors.

- Understand how to articulate a personal response to poems.

- Write, revise and perform own poem using personification and active verbs.

How you could plan this unit

Day 1	Day 2	Day 3	Day 4	Day 5
Reading	Writing	Reading	Writing	Reading and performing Perform own poems for class discussion
Poetic Personification	*Preparing to Write*	*Talking about Poems*	*Writing Your Own Poem*	

Poetic Personification

We will comment briefly on the success of *The Walrus and the Carpenter* poem. We will look at how the poet uses personification and active verbs. We will also be revising the word class 'verbs'

You need: Resource Pages A–C.

Whole class work

- Read and enjoy *The Walrus and the Carpenter* (Resource Page A) with the children. Ask for their first reactions.

- *Has anyone heard it before? Do you know of any other writing by Lewis Carroll? What makes it amusing? How did the poem make you feel? Which lines did you like best?*

- Display the first four verses of the poem and annotate (see Resource Page B). Explain personification and active verbs. Explain that writers can personify things through the use of personal pronouns (for example, 'he'/'she') or by describing them as having human emotions, appearance or abilities. Lewis Carroll uses all three in his poem:

> the sun shines with all its might — human ability
>
> the walrus wept — human emotion
>
> the oysters had their coats brushed and faces washed — human appearance.

- Explain that with active verbs the subject performs the action. Active verbs are better for listeners and therefore good to use in poetry because they are clearer, more direct and easier to understand.

Independent, pair or guided work

- Give out copies of the long extract (Resource Page C). Read through with the children.

- Ask them to identify and annotate active verbs and personification, using a different coloured pencil for each type of annotation.

Plenary

- Write these headings on the board:

> Human Ability / Human Emotion / Human Appearance

Ask the children to give you examples, from their annotations of the extract, that fit these subtitles.

- Ask the children to identify whether their example is used as an active verb in the text, for example, 'hopping' could imply human ability and is also an active verb.

- Kinaesthetic learners may wish to dramatise examples of active verbs.

- Read the poem through again for enjoyment.

Preparing to Write

Objective

We will be experimenting in using personification in our own writing

You need: Resource Page F.

Whole class work

- Review work on personification and active verbs from the previous lesson.

- Explain the plan for the rest of the week: the children will write their own sentences using active verbs and personification. Later they will experiment with these sentences by moving them around and revising the order to make a poem that they will perform aloud.

- Ask the children to brainstorm objects in the classroom and make a list of their suggestions on the board.

- Select one or two examples, explaining your choice, for example, 'I am going to choose items by which we can communicate, like a pen, a book or a piece of chalk.' Then model writing a short sentence using an active verb and personification for each one. Explain reasons for your choice as you write (see example 2, Resource Page F).

- Ask the children for their ideas for other objects in the classroom and script them. Keep a record of these to use for modelling how to organise sentences into a poem in a subsequent lesson.

Independent, paired or guided work

- Write two lists on the board:

- Ask the children to select a subject from list A and explore writing it in a sentence using personification. List B gives some examples but they could invent their own, for example 'The stone listens carefully to the daisies as they grow.'

- The children can continue to select different pairs of nouns and verbs – not necessarily the ones on the list.

A	B (active verbs)
sun	tells
moon	shows
stars	reminds
sky	teaches
sea	listens
stone	remembers
night	brings
mountain	looks
dawn	dances
morning	dreams
evening	guides

Plenary

- Each child reads one or two sentences to a response partner who identifies where personification is used.

13

Talking about Poems

Objective

We will learn how to justify our personal preference for a particular poem, and to explain how and why a poem affects the emotions of a reader

You need: Resource Pages D–F; large sheet of paper and marker pen for checklist.

Whole class work

- Tell the children that they are going to learn how to talk about poems.

- Explain that poems are written to communicate impressions and feelings, just like the lyrics of a song (poems set to music). For example, poems can make you feel sad, angry, calm, amused, inspired, reassured, or even numb.

- *Poems do not have to make strict sense – some poems are written to sound mysterious. Some will leave you with questions and wanting to find out more.*

- Read aloud and display the poem *The Mirror* (Resource Page D). Talk about the poem, including:
  - appropriateness of the title
  - word choice
  - understanding
  - use of poetic techniques such as simile, personification
  - use of active verbs
  - ease of reading aloud
  - rhythm and meter
  - overall opinion.

- Ask the children what you looked for in Sylvia Plath's poem and use their suggestions to put together a class checklist (see Resource Page F for ideas).

- Give out photocopies of the selection of additional poems (Resource Page E) and read aloud together.

Independent, pair or guided work

- Ask the children to select one of the poems. Referring to the pointers on the class checklist, they should make notes as they read it through in order to talk about their choice.

Plenary

- Select a child to talk about each of the chosen poems. Prompt a discussion with the rest of the class.
  - *Do you agree with these comments?*
  - *Did you find any other uses of poetic technique in the poem?*
  - *Do you like it or dislike it? Why?*
  - *How does it make you feel?*
  - *What do you think the poet was trying to communicate?*

Writing Your Own Poem

Objectives

We will be writing a poem experimenting with active verbs and personification. We will also revise poems for reading aloud individually

You need: Resource Pages F and G; children's suggestions from previous lesson, written on separate strips of paper; Post-it™ notes.

Whole class work

- Review the children's understanding of personification and active verbs.

- Reread their checklist for commenting about poems.

- Display the sentences about the classroom objects. Show the children how to select the order of the sentences to make a poem. Explain that they are 'selecting for the ear' – a poem that people will enjoy hearing as well as being able to read.

- *Listeners don't get a second chance – imagine you're hearing it on the radio. Readers who don't understand something can go back and read it again. Listeners can't. Listeners must understand your words the first time.*

- Model reading the arranged sentences aloud. Explain that when you read aloud you can hear problems that your eye doesn't notice, like sentences that are too long.

- Model rearranging the sentences. Model changing an active verb to get a better effect. Every time you make a change, read the poem aloud again.

- Ask the children to look away while you read a rearranged version. How much did they understand/hear when they couldn't see the words?

- Refer to the checklist for commenting about poems (Resource Page F). Ask for the children's opinion on your rearranged version. **What works? Why? Why not?**

Independent, pair or guided work

- Ask the children to select some of the sentences that they suggested earlier and write each one on a separate Post-it™ note.

- The children rearrange the Post-it™ notes and read the sentences aloud until they are satisfied with their poem.

- Encourage the children to edit sentences if necessary to improve the overall effect.

- They should refer to the marking ladder (Resource Page G) to ensure that they have included all the features.

Plenary

- The children read their poem to a response partner who explains how the poem makes them feel and what they particularly enjoyed about it. They could also suggest a way of improving a part of it, for example, by changing one of the verbs.

- The following lesson will be the performance of the poems. Suggest that the children work like professional announcers and news reporters by underlining words in their poem so they will remember to emphasise them by saying them louder or with more energy. They could make other marks to remember where they want to pause, or where to take a breath. Explain that it is rather like scoring a piece of music.

(Pupil copymaster)

The Walrus and The Carpenter by Lewis Carroll

The sun was shining on the sea,
Shining with all his might:
He did his very best to make
The billows smooth and bright –
And this was odd, because it was
The middle of the night.
The moon was shining sulkily,
Because she thought the sun
Had got no business to be there
After the day was done –
"It's very rude of him," she said,
"To come and spoil the fun!"

The sea was wet as wet could be,
The sands were dry as dry.
You could not see a cloud, because
No cloud was in the sky:
No birds were flying overhead –
There were no birds to fly.
The Walrus and the Carpenter
Were walking close at hand;
They wept like anything to see
Such quantities of sand:
"If this were only cleared away,"
They said, "it would be grand!"
"If seven maids with seven mops
Swept it for half a year.
Do you suppose," the Walrus said,
"That they could get it clear?"
"I doubt it," said the Carpenter,
And shed a bitter tear.
"O Oysters, come and walk with us!"
The Walrus did beseech.
"A pleasant walk, a pleasant talk,
Along the briny beach:
We cannot do with more than four,
To give a hand to each."
The eldest Oyster looked at him,
But never a word he said:
The eldest Oyster winked his eye,
And shook his heavy head –
Meaning to say he did not choose
To leave the oyster-bed.
But four young Oysters hurried up,
All eager for the treat:
Their coats were brushed, their faces washed,
Their shoes were clean and neat –
And this was odd, because, you know,
They hadn't any feet.
Four other Oysters followed them,
And yet another four;
And thick and fast they came at last,
And more, and more, and more –
All hopping through the frothy waves,
And scrambling to the shore.

The Walrus and the Carpenter
Walked on a mile or so,
And then they rested on a rock
Conveniently low:
And all the little Oysters stood
And waited in a row.
"The time has come," the Walrus said,
"To talk of many things:
Of shoes – and ships – and sealing-wax –
Of cabbages – and kings –
And why the sea is boiling hot –
And whether pigs have wings."
"But wait a bit," the Oysters cried,
"Before we have our chat;
For some of us are out of breath,
And all of us are fat!"
"No hurry!" said the Carpenter.
They thanked him much for that.
"A loaf of bread," the Walrus said,
"Is what we chiefly need:
Pepper and vinegar besides
Are very good indeed –
Now if you're ready, Oysters dear,
We can begin to feed."
"But not on us!" the Oysters cried,
Turning a little blue.
"After such kindness, that would be
A dismal thing to do!"
"The night is fine," the Walrus said.
"Do you admire the view?

"It was so kind of you to come!
And you are very nice!"
The Carpenter said nothing but
"Cut us another slice:
I wish you were not quite so deaf –
I've had to ask you twice!"
"It seems a shame," the Walrus said,
"To play them such a trick,
After we've brought them out so far,
And made them trot so quick!"
The Carpenter said nothing but
"The butter's spread too thick!"
"I weep for you," the Walrus said:
"I deeply sympathize."
With sobs and tears he sorted out
Those of the largest size,
Holding his pocket-handkerchief
Before his streaming eyes.
"O Oysters," said the Carpenter,
"You've had a pleasant run!
Shall we be trotting home again?'
But answer came there none –
And this was scarcely odd, because
They'd eaten every one.

Lewis Carroll, in Through the Looking Glass and What Alice Found There *(1872)*

(Exemplar analysis)

Example of analysis of *The Walrus and the Carpenter*

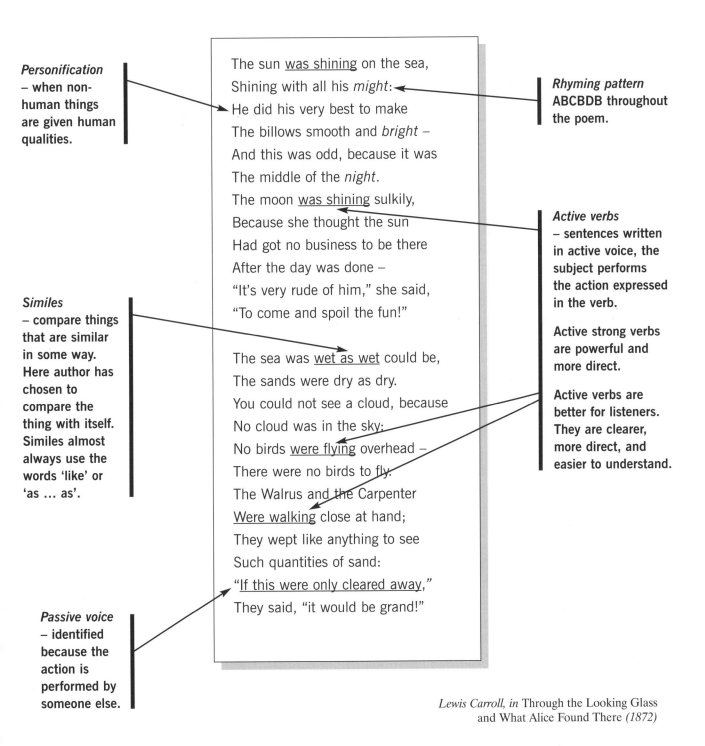

Personification
– when non-human things are given human qualities.

Rhyming pattern
ABCBDB throughout the poem.

The sun <u>was shining</u> on the sea,
Shining with all his *might*:
He did his very best to make
The billows smooth and *bright* –
And this was odd, because it was
The middle of the *night*.

The moon <u>was shining</u> sulkily,
Because she thought the sun
Had got no business to be there
After the day was done –
"It's very rude of him," she said,
"To come and spoil the fun!"

Active verbs
– sentences written in active voice, the subject performs the action expressed in the verb.

Active strong verbs are powerful and more direct.

Similes
– compare things that are similar in some way. Here author has chosen to compare the thing with itself. Similes almost always use the words 'like' or 'as … as'.

The sea was <u>wet as wet</u> could be,
The sands were dry as dry.
You could not see a cloud, because
No cloud was in the sky:
No birds <u>were flying</u> overhead –
There were no birds to fly.

The Walrus and the Carpenter
<u>Were walking</u> close at hand;
They wept like anything to see
Such quantities of sand:
"<u>If this were only cleared away</u>,"
They said, "it would be grand!"

Active verbs are better for listeners. They are clearer, more direct, and easier to understand.

Passive voice
– identified because the action is performed by someone else.

Lewis Carroll, in Through the Looking Glass
and What Alice Found There *(1872)*

(Pupil copymaster)

Extract from *The Walrus and the Carpenter*

The eldest Oyster looked at him,
But never a word he said:
The eldest Oyster winked his eye,
And shook his heavy head –
Meaning to say he did not choose
To leave the oyster-bed.
But four young Oysters hurried up,
All eager for the treat:
Their coats were brushed, their faces washed,
Their shoes were clean and neat –
And this was odd, because, you know,
They hadn't any feet.
Four other Oysters followed them,
And yet another four;
And thick and fast they came at last,
And more, and more, and more –
All hopping through the frothy waves,
And scrambling to the shore.

The Walrus and the Carpenter
Walked on a mile or so,
And then they rested on a rock
Conveniently low:
And all the little Oysters stood
And waited in a row.
"The time has come," the Walrus said,
"To talk of many things:
Of shoes – and ships – and sealing-wax –
Of cabbages – and kings –
And why the sea is boiling hot –
And whether pigs have wings."
"But wait a bit," the Oysters cried,
"Before we have our chat;
For some of us are out of breath,
And all of us are fat!"
"No hurry!" said the Carpenter.
They thanked him much for that.

Lewis Carroll, in Through the Looking Glass
and What Alice Found There *(1872)*

(Exemplar analysis)

Example of analysis of Sylvia Plath's *The Mirror*

Title:
good choice – helps the reader understand the subject of the poem. Appeals to the reader because probably every human has a bit of a vain streak and they want to know about a mirror.

Strong active verb.

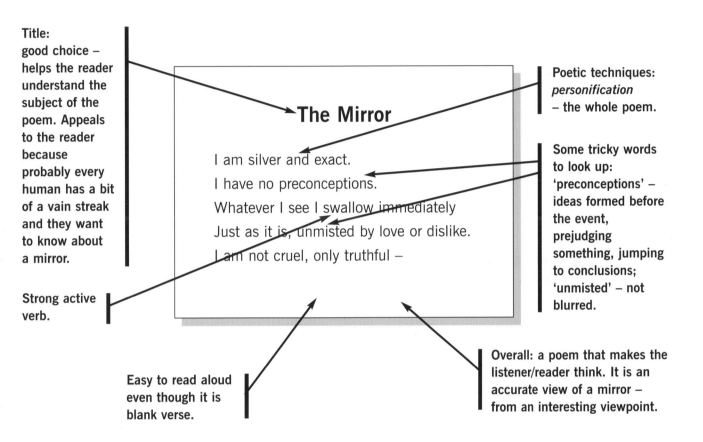

The Mirror

I am silver and exact.
I have no preconceptions.
Whatever I see I swallow immediately
Just as it is, unmisted by love or dislike.
I am not cruel, only truthful –

Poetic techniques:
personification – the whole poem.

Some tricky words to look up:
'preconceptions' – ideas formed before the event, prejudging something, jumping to conclusions; 'unmisted' – not blurred.

Easy to read aloud even though it is blank verse.

Overall: a poem that makes the listener/reader think. It is an accurate view of a mirror – from an interesting viewpoint.

(Pupil copymaster)

Additional poems

Two Sunflowers Move in the Yellow Room
by William Blake

"Ah, William, we're weary of weather,"
said the sunflowers, shining with dew.
"Our traveling habits have tired us.
Can you give us a room with a view?"
They arranged themselves at the window
and counted the steps of the sun,
and they both took root in the carpet
where the topaz tortoises run.

The Frowning Cliff
by Herbert Asquith

The sea has a laugh
And the cliff a frown
For the laugh of the sea
Is wearing him down

Lipping and lapping
Frown as he may
The laughing sea
will eat him away

Knees and body
And tawny head
He'll smile at last
On a golden bed.

Daffodils *by William Wordsworth*

I wander'd lonely as a cloud
That floats on high o'er vales and hills,
When all at once I saw a crowd,
A host, of golden daffodils;
Beside the lake, beneath the trees,
Fluttering and dancing in the breeze.

Continuous as the stars that shine
And twinkle on the Milky Way,
They stretch'd in never-ending line
Along the margin of a bay:
Ten thousand saw I at a glance,
Tossing their heads in sprightly dance.

The waves beside them danced; but they
Out-did the sparkling waves in glee:
A poet could not but be gay,
In such a jocund company:
I gazed – and gazed – but little thought
What wealth the show to me had brought:

For oft, when on my couch I lie
In vacant or in pensive mood,
They flash upon that inward eye
Which is the bliss of solitude;
And then my heart with pleasure fills,
And dances with the daffodils.

Fog *by Carl Sandburg*

The fog comes
on little cat feet.
It sits looking
over harbor and city
on silent haunches
and then moves on.

The Cat and the Fiddle
from Mother Goose, traditional

Hey diddle, diddle,
The cat and the fiddle,
The cow jumped over the moon;
The little dog laughed
To see such sport,
And the dish ran away with the spoon.

A Word is Dead
by Emily Dickinson

A word is dead
When it is said
Some say.
I say it just
Begins to live
That day.

(Exemplar analysis)

Checklist and model for poetry

Example of a checklist for commenting about poems ①

- Is the title appropriate for the subject? Does it generate interest and hint at what the poem is about?

- Who is talking?

- What is the poem talking about?

- How does it appeal to the reader? What emotions does it make you have?

- Is the word choice appropriate? Is it varied? Do you understand the words?

- Does the verb choice push the poem along? (Strong active verbs?)

- Are words repeated?

- Do they set the mood?

- Does the poet use simile, metaphor or personification? Do they help the poem?

- Is the rhythm natural, easy to read aloud?

- Is the rhyme pleasing?

- What is the overall impression?

Example of modelled writing using poetic personification ②

The pen walks across the paper.
'Walk' because the ideas are coming slowly.

The pen sprints across the paper.
As if someone was scribbling down ideas quickly.

The words in the book dance across the page.
The reader's mind is flitting from one idea to the other so the words are dancing.

The chalk squeaked as the teacher wrote the spellings.
Gives the impression that the chalk is not happy about this job.

(**Marking ladder**)

Name: _____

Pupil	Objective	Teacher
	I used an appropriate title that generates interest and hints at what my poem is about.	
	My word choice is appropriate for the subject and varied.	
	I used strong active verbs to push the poem along.	
	I used at least three examples of personification.	
	The rhythm is natural and easy to read aloud.	
	My choice of language makes it easy for a listener to understand.	
	What could I do to improve my work next time?	

Autobiography and Diaries

Outcome

Extract from an autobiography of a fictional character linked to history topic 'What was it like for children living in Victorian Britain?' (QCA Unit 11)

Objectives

Sentence

4 to investigate connecting words and phrases; to collect examples from reading and thesauruses; to study how points are typically connected in different kinds of text; to classify useful examples for different kinds of text, for example, by position; sequence; logic.

6 to secure knowledge and understanding of more sophisticated punctuation marks: colon; semi-colon; parenthetic commas, dashes, brackets.

Text

11 to distinguish between biography and autobiography:
- recognising the effect on the reader of the choice between first and third person
- distinguishing between fact, opinion and fiction
- distinguishing between implicit and explicit points of view and how these can differ.

14 to develop the skills of biographical and autobiographical writing in role, adopting distinctive voices, e.g. of historical characters.

17 to appraise a text quickly and effectively; to retrieve information from it; to find information quickly and evaluate its value.

Planning frame

- Read and analyse the features of autobiographical writing.
- Write the introduction to a fictional autobiographical account of an event.
- Skim and scan texts and make notes. Write the event.
- Write a reflective ending to the extract.

How you could plan this unit

Day 1	Day 2	Day 3	Day 4	Day 5
Reading	Writing	Reading	Writing Model and write event using a child's research	Writing
Identifying Features	*Setting the Scene*	*Research Techniques – Skimming and Scanning*		*Reflective Endings*

Day 6	Day 7
Reading Analyse diary texts and compare with autobiography checklist	Writing Teacher models a diary extract and children write own

Identifying Features

Objectives

We will identify the text and language features of an autobiographical text. We will make a collection of connecting words and phrases. We will also revise word classes: verbs and adjectives

You need: Resource Pages A–C; two large sheets of paper.

Whole class work	• Display the text *My Two Aunties* (Resource Page A) and read together.

• Ask the children to identify the genre (autobiography):

> 'auto' = referring to oneself
>
> 'biography' = story of a person's life

Brainstorm other autobiographical texts with which they are familiar: diaries, journals, letters, for example, Roald Dahl's *Boy*, or *The Diary of Anne Frank*.

• Annotate the text with features typical of autobiographical writing (see Resource Page B). Mention and explain:
  – orientation of the reader in the first paragraph
  – language to show time sequences
  – use of past tense and first person
  – detailed description of particular events using lively language and the inclusion of specific names to engage the reader
  – anecdotes
  – fact and opinion.

• After annotating, write the annotated time connectives and phrases on a large sheet of paper for classroom display.

Independent, pair or guided work

• Give out copies of *Pipe Dreams* (Resource Page C). Read together. Ask the children to annotate features that identify the text as autobiographical writing. They should also highlight time connectives.

Plenary

• Ask the children to add words to the time connective and phrases collection. Display the sheet for reference.

• Ask the children to tell you what features they have noticed in *Pipe Dreams*. As features are identified, list them on a class checklist and display it.

Setting the Scene

Objectives

We will write an opening to an autobiographical account. We will learn how to use time connectives and brackets and dashes. We will develop awareness of implicit and explicit points of view

You need: Resource Page D.

Whole class work

- Review the previous lesson's findings.

- Explain that today the children will start to write their own fictional autobiographical account of an event in the life of a Victorian child.

- Write two headings on the board: 'Setting/character' and 'Feelings'. Ask the children to brainstorm ideas to fit in each of these categories, for example:

Setting	Feelings
coal trap, boy in coalmine	fear

- Before modelling the first paragraph, tell the children that you are imagining you are an elderly person looking back on your life and writing about something that happened many years ago. Remind them about this again before they start their independent work.

- Model writing the first paragraph (Resource Page D), pointing out the features encountered in the previous lesson:
  - orientation of the reader through setting the scene, time and place
  - use of adjectives and adverbs to aid description and to keep the writing lively
  - inclusion of the writer's feelings
  - time connectives and phrases.

- Introduce the use of brackets to write an aside, and a dash to inject an element of surprise in the text.

- Ask the children what facts they know from the phrase in the modelled writing, 'Me – a gardener's boy' – that is, his sex, approximate age, the job he has.

- Then ask what else is inferred: that the writer did not think he could have such an important job when he left school, or he might be modest or have had problems with his education. Explain that the writer is using this as a hook to interest the reader. **What other hooks are there in the writing?** Answer: the relationship with his grandmother and sisters – what had happened to his parents?

Independent, pair or guided work

- Ask the children to select a setting from the brainstormed list. They can write the opening paragraph(s) of their account. Opening paragraphs should:
  - establish who, where and when
  - feature detailed description, including adjectives to engage the reader
  - feature lively writing
  - describe the writer's feelings

Plenary

- With response partners, the children read their introductions. They should decide what they know already about the character (explicit) and what they can read between the lines (implicit).

Research Techniques – Skimming and Scanning

Objectives

We will learn to skim and scan text to find relevant material. We will also practise writing notes to help write an event in our autobiography

You need: Resource Pages E–G; information books about the life of Victorian children; Post-it™ notes of varying sizes.

Whole class work

- Tell the children that they are going to learn how to find the information they need in order to write the rest of the autobiographical account.

- Brainstorm different sources of information about Victorian children.

- Review the use of chapter headings and indices in reference material.

- Model selecting relevant information from an information book.

- Explain that novels, TV dramas and documentaries could also be a source of information.

- Display the contents page from *Street Child* (Resource Page E). Skim down the page to find the chapter relevant to the workhouse.

> Skim = read or glance through quickly
>
> Scan = scrutinise in close detail

- Scan the extract from *Street Child* (Resource Page F) by reading it together.

- Model how to select the key points (Resource Page G):

> Skim down to find relevant paragraphs.
>
> Highlight key words.
>
> List main points on board.

Independent, pair or guided work

- Distribute relevant information books and novels for research and ask the children to use skimming and scanning to research their chosen option, noting the key points.

- To help the children improve their note-taking skills, writing only the key points, use Post-it™ notes. Each time they are required to make notes, give a smaller and smaller sized Post-it™ note but ask them to make a similar number of points.

Plenary

- Working in pairs, the children use their notes to tell each other three things they have found out. Select one child's notes, for example, about a chimney sweep's boy, to scribe on the board. Ask the children what they know *explicitly* from the notes, and what might be *implicit* or *inferred*?

- Give the children marking ladders for reference so that they include relevant points as they are writing up their chosen event for the autobiography.

Reflective Endings

Objectives

We will be concluding the extract from the autobiography with a reflective sentence. We will then review, edit and assess our own work

You need: Resource Pages H and I; modelled work from previous lessons.

Whole class work	• Read your modelled introduction and modelled event from previous lessons. Remind the children of the reflective statements used by Kit Wright and Raymond Briggs to conclude the extracts from *Pipe Dreams* and *My Two Aunties*: 'Which just goes to show ...' and 'Of course I am much nicer now.' • Model writing a few examples of reflective end statements to conclude your modelled writing (see example 3, Resource Page H). • Read aloud a child's work and ask the class for ideas of ways to conclude the writing. • Review the class checklist and marking ladder for autobiographical writing (Resource Page I).
Independent, pair or guided work	• The children write the concluding statements to their writing. Using response partners and the displayed checklist, the children identify the features and edit their writing.
Plenary	• The children reread their work and complete their marking ladder.

(Pupil copymaster)

My Two Aunties

When the war began I was five years old and had been evacuated to Dorset. Here I lived with two elderly aunties in a small stone cottage in the country. The walls were over two feet thick and the stone stairs curved steeply up beside the fireplace. The ceilings were so low that you could stand on the bottom stair and put something on the bedroom floor. The tiny bedroom windows were all at knee level.

There was no television, no tapes or CDs, no computer, no car, no shower, no bathroom, no central heating, no running hot water. Baths were taken in a tin tub in the kitchen. Except for the one coal fire in the living room there was no heating at all.

The lavatory was a corrugated iron shed under the apple tree. It did not flush. Inside it was a metal bucket containing disinfectant. It was called an Elsan. Mr Blake, a very poor farmer, used to be paid to come in and empty it once a month. He dug a hole and buried the contents under the apple tee. You were not allowed to pee in the Elsan as it would have filled up too quickly. I had to pee in the hedge.

The aunties always kept three suitcases ready-packed in case of invasion. If the Germans invaded we would have to flee westwards as refugees. One night, amid the drone of bombers overhead, there was a sudden roar of engines and a deafening burst of machine-gun fire. It sounded very close.

Aunt Betty shrieked, "Get the cases, Flo!" We hurried downstairs, pulled on coats over our pyjamas and nightdresses, seized the suitcases and stood there trembling. Quite where we were going on foot, in the middle of the night, was not clear.

In the end, we went nowhere and returned to bed, unharmed, but very frightened.

Once a week a bus came through the village about a mile away. We used to walk down to catch this bus and go into Shaftesbury to the shops. A big treat was to go to the pictures afterwards but we always had to leave before the film ended, in order to catch the one and only bus home.

It was on one of these shopping trips that I committed a dreadful offence which still embarrasses me today. I had lost a little toy in the garden and was very upset, as I'd paid sixpence for it. I even cried. Kind Auntie Flo said, "Never mind, dear. I'll get you something next week." So next Saturday she bought me a little toy costing fourpence.

I can still remember walking along the pavement beside her and wrestling with my conscience as I looked down at the pavement going past under my feet. I knew it was wrong but I had to say it. "You owe me tuppence!" I blurted out, and blushed with shame even as I said it. What a vile, ungrateful little beast I must have been!

Of course, I am much nicer today.

Raymond Briggs

(Exemplar analysis)

Example of analysis of *My Two Aunties*

Vocabulary/connectives showing time sequences (examples underlined).

Written in first person (pronoun 'I').

Introductory paragraph to set scene for reader – when, where, who etc.

Detailed description.

Use of names makes incidents come alive.

Anecdotes written in such a way as to make something serious seem amusing.

Writer's feelings.

Writer's reactions.

Opinion.

References to present day life to show how different it was then.

Anecdotes – short accounts of something interesting or humorous.

Powerful verbs make the writing lively.

Opinion.

Concluding statement gives a personal reflection on events.

When the war began I was five years old and had been evacuated to Dorset. Here I lived with two elderly aunties in a small stone cottage in the country. The walls were over two feet thick and the stone stairs curved steeply up beside the fireplace. The ceilings were so low that you could stand on the bottom stair and put something on the bedroom floor. The tiny bedroom windows were all at knee level.

There was no television, no tapes or CDs, no computer, no car, no shower, no bathroom, no central heating, no running hot water. Baths were taken in a tin tub in the kitchen. Except for the one coal fire in the living room there was no heating at all.

The lavatory was a corrugated iron shed under the apple tree. It did not flush. Inside it was a metal bucket containing disinfectant. It was called an Elsan. Mr Blake, a very poor farmer, used to be paid to come in and empty it once a month. He dug a hole and buried the contents under the apple tree. You were not allowed to pee in the Elsan as it would have filled up too quickly. I had to pee in the hedge.

The aunties always kept three suitcases ready-packed in case of invasion. If the Germans invaded we would have to flee westwards as refugees. One night, amid the drone of bombers overhead, there was a sudden roar of engines and a deafening burst of machine-gun fire. It sounded very close.

Aunt Betty shrieked, "Get the cases, Flo!" We hurried downstairs, pulled on coats over our pyjamas and nightdresses, seized the suitcases and stood there trembling. Quite where we were going on foot, in the middle of the night, was not clear.

In the end, we went nowhere and returned to bed, unharmed, but very frightened. Once a week a bus came through the village about a mile away. We used to walk down to catch this bus and go into Shaftesbury to the shops. A big treat was to go to the pictures afterwards but we always had to leave before the film ended, in order to catch the one and only bus home.

It was on one of these shopping trips that I committed a dreadful offence which still embarrasses me today. I had lost a little toy in the garden and was very upset, as I'd paid sixpence for it. I even cried. Kind Auntie Flo said, "Never mind, dear. I'll get you something next week." So next Saturday she bought me a little toy costing fourpence.

I can still remember walking along the pavement beside her and wrestling with my conscience as I looked down at the pavement going past under my feet. I knew it was wrong but I had to say it. "You owe me tuppence!" I blurted out, and blushed with shame even as I said it. What a vile, ungrateful little beast I must have been!

Of course, I am much nicer today.

Raymond Briggs

Pipe Dreams

Not many people nowadays smoke a pipe.

My father did. And he wasn't the only one. Many people smoked pipes of different shapes and sizes, from the ones which stuck out straight from the mouth, to the ones which bent like a slow snake. Well, they all seemed to like it, somehow, smoking a pipe.

For instance, I can remember a barge full of coal come chuntering down the Grand Union. That was the old canal beside whose banks we went to school. And steering this barge from the back was an old lady … her teeth clamped hard around a pipe! But nobody seemed to like it as much as my father. He puffed on it in the morning and he puffed on it in the evening. And if his pipe was already lit, he puffed on it in the lavatory. And this is my story.

One day he dropped his pipe down the lavatory bowl. Well! You'd think he might have thrown it away. Yuck! But no … this was his favourite pipe. So he picked it up, and he washed it out, and he soaked it for seven days in disinfectant. He soaked it so long the bowl of his pipe turned a rusty green. But it was clean! So he took it out and filled it. And he lit it. Well, I wasn't there but my brother was. He told me what happened next.

A giant green flame came leaping out of my father's pipe. It burned the ceiling and scorched his eyebrows. And apparently it didn't taste too good. "Good God!" he cried, as he sprang up from his chair. "Good God in Heaven!" and he danced round the room before throwing his pipe in the fire. Which goes to show a week's disinfectant is not the best thing to put in your pipe. Even if it is your favourite one.

Kit Wright

(Exemplar material)

Modelled introduction for an autobiography

Write this on the board ...	... while you are saying this
It was still dark	*Description of the time.*
when I	*First person.*
set off from Trevellyan Cottage in Perranwell,	*Where.*
on my long and gruelling	*Adjective.*
five-mile walk to Arwenack Manor.	*Setting the scene for the reader, using description to engage the reader.*
I was just eleven years old and it was my first day as gardener's boy in the big house. I had made this journey before, just one week ago, when I was interviewed by Lady Jane Godolphin.	*Event to give the reader a good understanding of what is going on, names to engage and bring it alive.*
Then I was so scared,	*Writer's feelings.*
I'm sure you could have heard my heart beating.	*Shows how scared he was.*
Now, I was feeling all mixed up inside, in such low spirits to be leaving my gran and sisters (well, maybe not Ellen because she was always so spiteful to me),	*Developing the idea of implicit and explicit points of view. Explain the use of brackets for an aside.*
but also so excited. Me – a gardener's boy.	*Dash to inject an element of surprise.*
Little did I know that within the year, the family would be bankrupt and I would be in the workhouse.	

(**Pupil copymaster**)

A contents page to skim

Skim to find *The Workhouse,* chapter 4, page 20

Contents

from Street Child, *by Berlie Doherty*

(Pupil copymaster)

Text to skim and scan – *Street Child*

Morning started with the six o'clock bell, when all the boys had to wash under the pump. Joseph watched them, swinging his head from side to side and bending his neck round like a hunched bird of prey. He kept flapping his arms across his bent chest to beat the cold away.

"Get yerselfs washed quick boys," he said. "Afore the wevver bites me bones off."

Across the yard from the pump was the asylum. Mad people were locked up. They wailed and shrieked for hours on end. They stretched their hands out through the bars of their prison. "Give us some bread, boy!" they begged. "Let me out! Let me out!"

(*Skimming shows that the next section just has more information about the asylum – not new information.*)

"Don't take no notice of them," a woolly-headed boy whispered to him one day. "They're mad. They're animals." Jim was shocked. He stared again at the men and women and children who were all squashed up together. Their cage was too small to hold them all. Their wailings echoed round the yard all the time. "Animals, animals," Jim said to himself, trying to drive their noises out of his head. He looked away from them, pretending they weren't there.

"No, they're not animals, Jim," Joseph told him. "They're people, they are. People, Jim. My ma's in there."

There was a shed at the other end of the yard. Boys gazed out at them through a small barred window. Their white faces were even more frightening than the wailings of mad people. Joseph sidled over to Jim that first morning and swung his arm across the boy's shoulder, bringing his head round to mutter down Jim's ear. "Now, them's the boys what tries to run away. They catch 'em and beat 'em and stick 'em in there till they're good. Remember that."

After the cold wash in the yard Jim had to help to clean it out with brooms twice as tall as he was. They had to sweep it till the ground was bare and clean, even if hundreds of leaves had fallen in the night and come drifting over the high walls. At breakfast the boys queued up with their bowls in their hands for bread and tea. The bread was meant to last for every meal, but if Jim tried to save it he soon had it stolen by one of the older boys. He learnt to gulp down his food as quickly as they did; boiled meat at dinner time, cheese at night, all swallowed rapidly and in silence.

from Street Child, *by Berlie Doherty*

(Exemplar analysis)

Example of skim and scan of *Street Child*

Morning started with the six o'clock bell, when all the boys had to wash under the pump. Joseph watched them, swinging his head from side to side and bending his neck round like a hunched bird of prey. He kept flapping his arms across his bent chest to beat the cold away.

"Get yerselfs washed quick boys," he said. "Afore the wevver bites me bones off."

Across the yard from the pump was the asylum. Mad people were locked up. They wailed and shrieked for hours on end. They stretched their hands out through the bars of their prison. "Give us some bread, boy!" they begged. "Let me out! Let me out!"

(*Skimming shows that the next section just has more information about the asylum – not new information.*)

"Don't take no notice of them," a woolly-headed boy whispered to him one day. "They're mad. They're animals." Jim was shocked. He stared again at the men and women and children who were all squashed up together. Their cage was too small to hold them all. Their wailings echoed round the yard all the time. "Animals, animals," Jim said to himself, trying to drive their noises out of his head. He looked away from them, pretending they weren't there.

"No, they're not animals, Jim," Joseph told him. "They're people, they are. People, Jim. My ma's in there."

There was a shed at the other end of the yard. Boys gazed out at them through a small barred window. Their white faces were even more frightening than the wailings of mad people. Joseph sidled over to Jim that first morning and swung his arm across the boy's shoulder, bringing his head round to mutter down Jim's ear. "Now, them's the boys what tries to run away. They catch 'em and beat 'em and stick 'em in there till they're good. Remember that."

After the cold wash in the yard Jim had to help to clean it out with brooms twice as tall as he was. They had to sweep it till the ground was bare and clean, even if hundreds of leaves had fallen in the night and come drifting over the high walls. At breakfast the boys queued up with their bowls in their hands for bread and tea. The bread was meant to last for every meal, but if Jim tried to save it he soon had it stolen by one of the older boys. He learnt to gulp down his food as quickly as they did; boiled meat at dinner time, cheese at night, all swallowed rapidly and in silence.

from Street Child, *by Berlie Doherty*

Write these notes on the board as you highlight the text

- 6am – wash at pump in yard
- Near asylum where mad locked up – wails and screams all day
- Escapers locked up at other end of yard, beaten
- Job to sweep yard clean of leaves
- Bread ration at breakfast to last all day, stolen by older boys, so ate quickly. Meat for dinner, cheese for tea

From the notes, decide possible events to be written in the autobiography

- Bullied by older boys, stealing bread incident
  or
- Managed to escape from the workhouse
  or
- Was caught escaping and put in the prison at the end of the yard

Classworks Literacy Year 6 © Paula Ross, Nelson Thornes Ltd 2003

(Exemplar material)

Checklists and model for autobiography and diaries

Example of a checklist for autobiographical writing

- The writer is the main character

- Written in the first person

- Recounts key incidents in the writer's life

- Reveals the writer's feelings, reactions, values and goals

- Generally in chronological order

- Uses past tense to describe events

- Can have an informal tone

Example of a checklist for diary writing

- List events in chronological order

- Write in the first person and past tense

- Use a chatty style

- Can use own abbreviations

- Reveal your feelings and opinions

Example of modelled end statements for an autobiography

I'll never forget the day that I saw the back of the workhouse for good.
A lasting impression

From then on I could never look Charlie in the eyes.
A consequence

Looking back I can see it would never have worked. I was just too little to reach the keys.
A re-evaluation

Marking ladder

Name: _____

Pupil	Objective	Teacher
	I have written a clear opening paragraph for my extract to set the scene.	
	I have used first person pronouns consistently.	
	I have written in the past tense.	
	I have included my feelings, reactions and opinions.	
	My writing is about events that were important to me.	
	I have used at least three connectives and phrases to indicate time.	
	I have included detailed description using powerful verbs and adjectives.	
	I have concluded my extract with a reflection.	
	What could I do to improve my work next time?	

Biographical Writing

Outcome

Biography of a mountaineer, using ICT (cross-curricular link to QCA Unit 15 'The Mountain Environment')

Objectives

Sentence

2 to revise earlier work on verbs and to understand the terms 'active' and 'passive'; being able to transform a sentence from active to passive, and vice versa.

3 to note and discuss how changes from active to passive affect the word order and sense of a sentence.

5 to form complex sentences through, e.g.: using different connecting devices; reading back complex sentences for clarity of meaning and adjusting as necessary; evaluating which links work best; exploring how meaning is affected by sequence and structure of clauses.

Text

11 to distinguish between biography and autobiography: recognising the effect on the reader of the choice between first and third person; distinguishing between fact, opinion and fiction; distinguishing between implicit and explicit points of view and how these can differ.

14 to develop the skills of biographical and autobiographical writing in role, adopting distinctive voices.

17 to appraise a text quickly and effectively; to retrieve information from it; to find information quickly and evaluate its value.

18 to use IT to plan, revise, edit writing to improve accuracy and conciseness and to bring it to publication standard.

Planning frame

- Read and analyse the features of biographical writing.
- The children write introduction to biography of a mountaineer.
- Make a time line using interview with mountaineer **http://www.bonington.com.**
- Model and write a plan from the time line. Model and write link sentences.
- Read, analyse, model and write concluding paragraph for biography.

How you could plan this unit

Day 1	Day 2	Day 3	Day 4	Day 5
Reading	Writing	Reading Skimming and scanning for research (could be taught in Geography)	Writing	Reading/Writing
Types and Features	*Rhetorical Openings*		*A Planning Frame*	*Concluding Paragraphs*

Day 6	Day 7	Day 8
Writing Use of the passive voice. Continue writing the biography	Writing Complete the biography. Final edit. Complete marking ladder	Reading Share biographies/ autobiographies and diary extracts for comparison. Compare checklists

Types and Features

Objectives

We will identify and annotate the text and language features of a biographical text. We will come to understand that biographies include facts and opinions and be able to identify both

You need: Resource Pages A–C and H; display paper.

Whole class work

- Display the biography of Judy Blume (Resource Page A) and read together.

- Ask the children to identify the genre. Discuss the different types of biographies available:

  - Biographical encyclopedia – facts and generally held opinion, for example, Isambard Kingdom Brunel was one of the world's best engineers.

  - Directory of famous people, like Who's Who? – lists names, addresses and their main achievements, but doesn't include opinion.

  - Entire book about one person written with the permission of the subject (authorised biography) – includes chosen facts and doesn't necessarily cover the subject's entire life.

  - Entire book about one person written without the subject's permission (unauthorised biography) – may be written from a particular point of view, therefore could be biased. Will include many opinions as well as facts.

  - Non-fiction book about a person organised in 'chapters', for example the Great Lives series — mainly facts with some generally held opinions.

  - Web sites are a good source of biographies, for example, http://www.acs.ucalgary.ca/~dkbrown/authors.html, Children's Literature Web Guide, which includes authors' personal web sites and web sites maintained by fans, scholars and readers. The amount of fact and opinion will vary depending on the writer of the biography.

- Annotate the text with features typical of biographical writing (see Resource Page B). Mention and explain:
  - opening paragraph can briefly summarise the person's life
  - written in the past tense and third person
  - recounts key incidents in the subject's life
  - events are usually written in chronological order but with some general explanatory paragraphs
  - use of the passive tense gives a formality to the writing.

Independent, pair or guided work

- The children analyse and annotate the biography of the Captain of the *Titanic* (Resource Page C).

- Others might use a search engine to find the biographies of characters pertinent to topics being studied by the class. These could be used for analysis and annotation.

Plenary

- Ask the children to offer suggestions of features found in a biography. Write these on display paper as the start of a class checklist for biographical writing (see Resource Page H for ideas).

Rhetorical Openings

Objectives

We will write an opening to an autobiographical account, using a rhetorical question

You need: Resource Page D; access to computers for children's writing; Post-it™ notes.

Whole class work

- Review the previous lesson's findings about the genre.

- Discuss the need to hook the reader in the introductory paragraph. Read the extract about Roald Dahl (Resource Page D). Explain that the writer has used a device called a rhetorical question.

> Rhetorical questions are not answered by the writer, because the answer is obvious, and usually just a yes or no.
>
> They can be used for effect, emphasis, or provocation, or to infer a conclusion.
>
> Often the rhetorical question and its implied answer will lead to further discussion.
>
> Several rhetorical questions together can form a nicely developed and directed paragraph by changing a series of statements into queries.

- Display Chris Bonington's CV from the web site **http://www.bonington.com**. Through questioning, show how Bonington is one of the world's greatest mountaineers.

- Model the writing of possible rhetorical questions to start the introductory paragraph of the biography (Resource Page D).

- *How do you think your questions might hook a reader?*

- Explain that the finished biography will be presented as a leaflet for an exhibition about the sport of mountain climbing. Demonstrate how to select an appropriate template from desk top publishing software.

Independent, pair or guided work

- Ask the children to orally rehearse possible rhetorical questions for the introductory paragraph of a biography with a partner before writing into the template.

- Remind the children to continually review their work and reread aloud their sentences to make sure the writing flows and makes sense.

Plenary

- With a response partner, read each other's introductions. Using Post-it™ notes, each partner writes a positive point and suggests a way to improve something in the introduction, for example, select a more powerful verb. The writer could then edit the sentence to make better sense.

A Planning Frame

Objectives

We will use the time line of Chris Bonington's life to make and complete a planning frame for the biography. We will also investigate linking phrases and words to move from one paragraph to the next

You need: Resource Page H; time line of events in life of Chris Bonington; display paper.

Whole class work

- Explain that today you are going to plan a framework to help you write the biography.

- Review checklist 1 (Resource Page H) to establish that biographies are generally chronological.

- Model the planning of a framework:

Introduction summarises the person's life	Events as a child and teenager	Main achievements	Events up to present day (or death)	Conclusion: the effect of this person's

- Display a time line and ask, **Which events do you think would fit into the 'childhood' section of the biography?** Write these into the planning frame.

- Ask the children to refer to the timeline and decide how many events would fit into 'Main achievements'. Suggest that they organise this section further, writing one general paragraph about his climbs and then a more detailed account of a particular climb, for example, the Ogre in 1977.

- Explain the necessity of finding different ways of starting sentences to ensure the biography is more than a list of achievements. This can be done by using a variety of linking phrases and words, for example:

> In addition ... Moreover ... Furthermore ... Nevertheless ... Later ... Eventually ... In the year ...

- Model writing a linking sentence to move from the introduction to the 'Childhood' section of the biography, using one of the phrases above.

Independent, pair or guided work

- The children prepare a planning framework and enter relevant facts from their research into each section.

Plenary

- The children suggest linking words and phrases. Scribe their ideas on to a sheet of paper for display. Select one or two examples of the phrases and ask the children for ways they might use these in a sentence about Chris Bonington.

Concluding Paragraphs

Objectives

We will write the final paragraph of the biography. We will also learn to distinguish between fact, opinion and fiction

You need: Resource Pages E–H; access to computers for children's writing.

Whole class work

- Read and analyse a selection of concluding paragraphs from biographies (Resource Page E). Mention the need to include details that sum up the person's character as this will have affected their life and degree of success. Add something about their importance in their field and how they will be remembered. Discuss the use of fact and opinion in this paragraph (see Resource Page F).

- Build a class checklist for the final paragraph (see checklist 2, Resource Page H for ideas).

- Model the writing of a concluding paragraph for the Bonington biography (Resource Page G).

- Ask the children to identify the fact and opinion in the paragraph.

Independent, pair or guided work

- The children write their concluding paragraphs. Encourage them to orally rehearse sentences before writing.

- Presenting this work using ICT gives the children the advantage that they can write their points down in any order without the need to rewrite at the end of the composing time.

Plenary

- Select one or two examples of the children's work and ask them to read the final paragraph aloud. Ask the rest of the class to identify any features from the checklist. If a feature is absent, encourage the class to suggest ways of developing this aspect.

Judy Blume – The Official Bio

Judy Blume spent her childhood in Elizabeth, New Jersey, making up stories inside her head. She has spent her adult years in many places, doing the same thing, only now she writes her stories down on paper. Adults as well as children will recognize such Blume titles as: *Are You There God? It's Me, Margaret*; *Superfudge*; *Blubber*; *Just As Long As We're Together*; and *Forever*. She has also written the novels *Wifey*, *Smart Women*, and her latest, *Summer Sisters*, the New York Times No. 1 bestseller. More than 75 million copies of her books have been sold, and her work has been translated into twenty-something languages. She receives thousands of letters a month from readers of all ages who share their feelings and concerns with her. Judy received a BSc in education from New York University in 1961, which named her a Distinguished Alumna in 1996, the same year the American Library Association honoured her with the Margaret A Edwards Award for Lifetime Achievement. She has won more than ninety awards, none more important than those coming directly from her youngest readers.

She is the founder and trustee of The Kids Fund, a charitable and educational foundation. She serves on the boards of the Authors' Guild; the Society of Children's Book Writers and Illustrators, where she sponsors an award for contemporary fiction; and the National Coalition Against Censorship, working to protect intellectual freedom. Recently, she edited *Places I Never Meant To Be, Original Stories by Censored Writers*. Currently, she is working on a book about the irrepressible Fudge.

Judy lives on islands up and down the East Coast with her husband George Cooper, who writes non-fiction. They have three grown children and one incredible grandchild.

see http://www.judyblume.com

Classworks Literacy Year 6 © Paula Ross, Nelson Thornes Ltd 2003

Exemplar analysis

Example of analysis of Judy Blume's bio

Past tense.

3rd person pronoun.

Present tense because this is something which still happens.

Recounts key incidents in the subject's life.

Fact.

Judy Blume spent her childhood in Elizabeth, New Jersey, making up stories inside her head. She has spent her adult years in many places, doing the same thing, only now she writes her stories down on paper. Adults as well as children will recognize such Blume titles as: *Are You There God? It's Me, Margaret*; *Superfudge*; *Blubber*; *Just As Long As We're Together*; and *Forever*. She has also written the novels *Wifey*, *Smart Women*, and her latest, *Summer Sisters*, the New York Times No. 1 bestseller. More than 75 million copies of her books have been sold, and her work has been translated into twenty-something languages. She receives thousands of letters a month from readers of all ages who share their feelings and concerns with her. Judy received a BSc in education from New York University in 1961, which named her a Distinguished Alumna in 1996, the same year the American Library Association honoured her with the Margaret A Edwards Award for Lifetime Achievement. She has won more than ninety awards, none more important than those coming directly from her youngest readers.

She is the founder and trustee of The Kids Fund, a charitable and educational foundation. She serves on the boards of the Authors' Guild; the Society of Children's Book Writers and Illustrators, where she sponsors an award for contemporary fiction; and the National Coalition Against Censorship, working to protect intellectual freedom. Recently, she edited *Places I Never Meant To Be, Original Stories by Censored Writers*. Currently, she is working on a book about the irrepressible Fudge.

Judy lives on islands up and down the East Coast with her husband George Cooper, who writes non-fiction. They have three grown children and one incredible grandchild.

see http://www.judyblume.com

First paragraph gives the reader a summary of her life.

3rd person pronoun.

Passive voice adds formality.

Events are written in chronological order – see also first paragraph details about childhood.

Opinion.

As she is still alive the references to what she will be remembered for and her importance as a writer are either told or inferred in the text.

(Pupil copymaster)

Edward John Smith, Captain of the *Titanic*

CAPTAIN EDWARD JOHN SMITH (age 62) was born at Hanley, Stoke-on-Trent, England on January 27th, 1850 – the son of potter Edward Smith and his wife Catherine. Edward John Smith attended the Etruria British School until the age of 13 when he went to Liverpool to begin a seafaring career as an apprentice on a clipper ship – the Senator Weber owned by Gibson & Co. – in 1869.

He joined the White Star Line in 1880 as Fourth Officer and gained his first command in 1887. Among the ships he would command were the first *Republic*, *Coptic*, *Majestic*, *Baltic*, *Adriatic* and *Olympic*. In total he captained 17 White Star liners.

On January 13th, 1887 he married Sarah Eleanor Pennington at St Oswald's Church, Winwick. Their daughter Helen Melville Smith, known as Mel, was born in Liverpool and later moved to Southampton with her parents. The family lived in an imposing red-brick, twin-gabled house 'Woodhead' on Winn Road, Westwood, Southampton. Captain Smith soon became a master seaman, and was considered the top dog in the formidable White Star Line's fleet. He often took the company's ships out on their sea trials and their first voyages. His capability and experience attracted a lot of people to him. Many of the White Star Line employees would request to be transferred to whatever ship he was captaining at the time in order to be near the 'millionaires Captain'.

Prior to the disaster, Captain Smith had captained the *Olympic*, *Titanic*'s sister ship, for almost a year. All in all, Captain Smith had 46 years of experience on the sea, including captaining a ship during the Boer war. Sadly, he planned to retire after Titanic's maiden voyage.

*see **http://www.euronet.nl/users/keesree/captain.htm#General***

Examples of rhetorical openings

Have you ever heard of Fantastic Mr Fox? Or read about the enormous crocodile? Do you know what was scary about The Magic Finger? If you say yes to these questions then you are probably a fan of Roald Dahl already. If you say no, don't worry … it means you are in for a treat! For Roald Dahl was one of the most successful writers for children who ever lived. This is his story.

Have you ever imagined what it would be like to climb the world's highest mountains? To live with fear and excitement all your life, to be honoured by countries all over the planet? To receive a knighthood from the Queen? One man has done just that, Sir Chris Bonington. This is his story.

Examples of concluding paragraphs

When Isambard Kingdom Brunel died in London on 15th September, 1859, the world lost one of its truly great engineering masters.

http://www.britainexpress.com/History/bio/brunel.htm

During Victoria's reign, Britain expanded into an empire. Victoria became an icon and symbol of her age. Queen Victoria died in 1901, at the age of 81. She had left elaborate instructions for her funeral. As she had wished, her own sons lifted her into the coffin. She wore a white dress and her wedding veil. Because Victoria had disliked black funerals, London was festooned in purple and white. She was buried beside Prince Albert in the Frogmore Royal Mausoleum at Windsor Castle. Victoria had reigned for nearly 64 years – the longest reign in British history.

http://www.royalty.nu/Europe/England/Victoria.html

Instead with that dramatic free kick, he had secured the 2–2 draw with Greece which guaranteed that England would be playing in Japan and Korea in 2002. And in doing so he had become the saviour of England and a hero for the nation.

from This is David Beckham – Portrait of a Superstar *(Scholastic)*

(Exemplar analysis)

Example of analysis of concluding paragraphs

A generally held opinion about the importance of the character and how he will be remembered.

> When Isambard Kingdom Brunel died in London on 15th September, 1859, the world lost one of its truly great engineering masters.
>
> *http://www.britainexpress.com/History/bio/brunel.htm*

Gives a fact.

Interesting information to continue to engage the reader.

Tells her influence in the world.

Final sentence gives a fact that reinforces the idea of her influence lasting a long time. This is a factual account.

> During Victoria's reign, Britain expanded into an empire. Victoria became an icon and symbol of her age. Queen Victoria died in 1901, at the age of 81. She had left elaborate instructions for her funeral. As she had wished, her own sons lifted her into the coffin. She wore a white dress and her wedding veil. Because Victoria had disliked black funerals, London was festooned in purple and white. She was buried beside Prince Albert in the Frogmore Royal Mausoleum at Windsor Castle. Victoria had reigned for nearly 64 years – the longest reign in British history.
>
> *http://www.royalty.nu/Europe/England/Victoria.html*

Gives an impression of her importance and how she will be remembered.

This is Victoria's opinion not the writer adding his or her own opinion.

Opinion.

Suggest that an author needs to be aware who readers of the biography might be when choosing the phrasing of sentences, word choice and so on.

How he will be remembered.

> Instead with that dramatic free kick, he had secured the 2–2 draw with Greece which guaranteed that England would be playing in Japan and Korea in 2002. And in doing so he had become the saviour of England and a hero for the nation.
>
> *from* This is David Beckham – Portrait of a Superstar *(Scholastic)*

Gives a picture of his importance. This is an opinion particular to football fans.

(Exemplar material)

Example of modelling a concluding paragraph

Write this on the board ...	... while you are saying this
It all started for Chris, when he read W H Murray's book about mountains.	*Initially write the sentence. Then rearrange with 'For Chris' at the start, explaining that this gives the sentence a more powerful start, emphasising the subject.*
For Chris, it all started when he read W H Murray's book about mountains.	*A link sentence into the paragraph.*
Then his heart was set	*Passive voice.*
on a dream to be a great mountaineer.	*Reminds the reader of what he set out to do.*
Not only	*Vary the sentence starts for interest.*
has he succeeded but his courage, determination and leadership	*Sum up his character.*
have made him	*Passive voice.*
one of the greatest mountaineers ever to live.	*His importance in the field of mountaineering and what he will be remembered for.*
Would you have the courage to succeed as this remarkable man has done?	*Relates the subject to the reader in a well-drawn conclusion to the paragraph. Uses a rhetorical question.*

Exemplar material

Checklists for biographical writing

Example of a checklist for biographical writing ①

- Ensure that the opening sentence hooks the reader

- Use the opening paragraph to briefly summarise the person's life

- Write in the third person

- Write in the past tense

- Use the passive voice to make the writing more formal

- Recount key incidents in the subject's life

- Write events in chronological order but with some general explanatory paragraphs

- Use paragraphs to sequence events

Example of a checklist for a concluding paragraph ②

- Sum up the person's character

- State their importance in their field

- State how they will be remembered

- Introduce new facts if desired

- Include an opinion

- Relate the subject to the reader by finishing with a question

Marking ladder

Name: _____

Pupil	Objective	Teacher
	I have used a rhetorical question to hook the reader.	
	My first paragraph summarises the main event(s) of the person's life.	
	I have used third person pronouns consistently.	
	I have written in the past tense.	
	I have used the passive voice to make the writing more formal.	
	My work is about key events in the person's life.	
	I have used at least three different ways of linking sentences or paragraphs: 1 2 3	
	My final paragraph mentions something about the person's • main achievements • personality • how he/she will be remembered.	
	What could I do to improve my biographical writing next time?	

Classic Fiction: Treasure Island

Outcome

A summary of R.L. Stevenson's text in a specified number of words; an extract with two narrators; a narration of a modern version of a quest story; an extract written in the style and voice of the text; a playscript of an extract

This is a five-week unit (as suggested in DfES Year 6 Planning Exemplification 1). The children should be familiar with the story before commencing.

Objectives

Sentence

1 to revise from Y5: the different word classes; re-expressing sentences in a different order; the construction of complex sentences; the conventions of standard English; adapting texts for particular readers and purposes.

4 to investigate connecting words and phrases: collect examples from reading and thesauruses; study how points are typically connected in different kinds of text; classify useful examples for different kinds of text, e.g., by position ('besides', 'nearby', 'by'); sequence ('firstly', 'secondly' ...); logic ('therefore', 'so', 'consequently'); identify connectives which have multiple purposes (e.g. 'on', 'under', 'besides').

5 to form complex sentences through, e.g.: using different connecting devices; reading back complex sentences for clarity of meaning, and adjusting as necessary; evaluating which links work best; exploring how meaning is affected by the sequence and structure of clauses.

6 to secure knowledge and understanding of more sophisticated punctuation marks: colon; semi-colon; parenthetic commas, dashes, brackets.

Text

2 to take account of viewpoint in a novel through, e.g.: identifying the narrator; explaining how this influences the reader's view of events; explaining how events might look from a different point of view.

3 to articulate personal responses to literature, identifying why and how a text affects the reader.

4 to be familiar with the work of some established authors, to know what is special about their work, and to explain their preferences in terms of authors, styles and themes.

5 to contribute constructively to shared discussion about literature responding to and building on the views of others.

6 to manipulate narrative perspective by: writing in the voice and style of a text; producing a modern retelling; writing a story with two different narrators.

7 to plan quickly and effectively the plot, characters and structure of their own narrative writing.

8 to summarise a passage chapter or text in a specified number of words.

9 to prepare a short section of story as a script, e.g. using stage directions, location/setting.

Planning frame

- Understand the structure of non-contemporary fiction and employ the style for own fiction.

Notes

- Children need to hear the story before the work on this unit commences. Listening to an audio version is an effective way of doing this:
  - the story is slightly abridged
  - the actor reading the text is able to use different but consistent voices for each character
  - chapters or sections can be replayed for more intensive study.
- Abridged texts of *Treasure Island* can be found in compendiums of classic texts for children. Ladybird also produce a version. This type of text may be more accessible for lower ability children.
- On Day 18, children watch the beginning of the film set at The Admiral Benbow.
- On Day 19 they will watch the ending (from the time when the pirates arrive at the place where they think they will find the treasure).
- It is possible to write the film review on Day 20 from these two extracts but it may be more effective if children are able to view the rest of the film by Day 20.

Resources

- Book: *Treasure Island*, by Robert Louis Stevenson (Wordsworth Editions Ltd, 1993, ISBN 1853261033)
- Film: *Treasure Island* (Disney 1950) or *Treasure Island* (MGM, 1934, black and white).
- Audio: *Treasure Island* (Naxos AudioBooks, 1996, ISBN 9626341017)
- Also available in **e-book**.

Key chapters

Chapter	1	All elements of the story are established
Chapter	2	Dialogue
Chapter	3	One of the most action-packed chapters of the book
Chapter	5	First battle between good and evil
Chapter	6	Building suspense
Chapter	8	Introduces Long John Silver
Chapter	10	Building suspense
Chapter	11	Dialogue
Chapter	12	About the narrator
Chapter	13	Setting
Chapter	14	Description
Chapter	18	A ship's log
Chapter	19	Narrator
Chapter	20	Setting
Chapter	22	Description, similes and metaphors
Chapter	23	Figurative language
Chapter	28	The changing character of Jim Hawkins
Chapter	29	Dialogue

How you could plan this unit

Day 1	Day 2	Day 3	Day 4	Day 5
Reading and analysis	**Modelling and writing**	**Reading and analysis**	**Writing**	**Reading and analysis** Read character summaries, annotate own pictures of the characters
Summaries	*Writing a Summary*	*Planning Frames*	*Planning a Quest Story*	

Day 6	Day 7	Day 8	Day 9	Day 10
Reading and analysis	**Modelling/role play/writing**	**Reading and analysis** Read and analyse settings from chapters 1, 14, 20, 22	**Modelling and writing** Plan setting and characters of own story for retelling	**Reading/analysis/role play**
Understanding Dialogue	*Writing a Dialogue*			*The Narrator*

Day 11	Day 12	Day 13	Day 14	Day 15
Modelling and writing	**Writing** Plan, write notes and rehearse using two narrators in their own story for retelling	**Reading and analysis**	**Modelling and writing**	**Writing, speaking and listening** Plan and write notes for ending. Rehearse stories for retelling.
Different Viewpoints		*Dilemma and Resolution*	*Features of Stevenson's Style*	

Day 16	Day 17	Day 18	Day 19	Day 20
Speaking and listening Rehearse the story adding links. Edit	**Speaking and listening** In groups, present modern retelling of the story to each other. Choose one to retell to the class	**Watching and analysis** View extract from the beginning of the film of *Treasure Island*. Analyse differences from the book	**Watching and analysis** View extract from the ending of the film. Analyse differences from the book	**Reading, analysis, modelling**
				Film Reviews

Day 21	Day 22	Day 23	Day 24	Day 25
Reading, analysis, modelling and role play	**Modelling, role play and analysis**	**Writing** Continue writing the extract as a playscript	**Reading and analysis** Review and analyse book reviews	**Modelling and writing** Write a review of *Treasure Island* in 50–75 words for a web page
Narrative into Playscript	*Writing a Playscript*			

Summaries

Objectives

We will become familiar with the work of Robert Louis Stevenson and find out what is special about it. We will be able to contribute constructively to shared discussion about the book. We will also explore and annotate the features of a summary

You need: Resource Pages A–E and GG.

Whole class work

- Explain that this is the start of a unit based around the story of *Treasure Island*, which they have been listening to. *You are going to use the writing of Robert Louis Stevenson to help you plan and write a variety of pieces including a summary, a play script and a film review, and you will be involved in planning and telling a modern version of a Treasure Island story.*

- *You can use the summary to explore and analyse the whole story – a good summary gives the text in a condensed form. It should be as accurate as possible and give the full sense of the original story.*

- *Reading a summary helps to give you a better grasp and understanding of all that happens.*

- Display the OHT of the summary (Resource Pages A and B). Explain that the summary comes from a web site and that many summaries of books can be found on the Internet.

- Use the annotated example (Resource Pages C and D) to point out the features of a summary including:
  - the importance of stating the author's name in the first sentence
  - chronological order and use of connectives
  - factual account, does not offer the 'summariser's' opinions or feelings
  - reducing the detail of the chapter to just one or two main points.

- *Do you feel the 'summariser' here has rephrased the author's words without changing their meaning, or the order or balance of the original work?*

- The text is very useful for examples of complex and compound sentence structures for sentence work.

Independent, pair or guided work

- Distribute an alternative summary of the book (Resource Page E). The children highlight the features noted from the shared work.

- *Does the summary cover the whole story? If not, what is missed out? Where would you find a book summary that doesn't give away the plot?* (Answer: a book blurb.)

Plenary

- Ask the children to offer suggestions for the features found in a summary. Write these on a whiteboard as the start of a class checklist (see checklist 1, Resource Page EE for ideas).

Writing a Summary

Objective

We will write a summary of chapter 1 of *Treasure Island* in approximately 100 words

You need: Resource Pages F–H and EE; large sheet of display paper; Post-it™ notes.

Whole class work

- Review the previous lesson's findings about a summary. Explain that the outcome of today's work will be a summary of chapter 1. *In chapter 1, Stevenson manages to establish all the elements of the subsequent action.*

- Listen to chapter 1 again (if using the CD-ROM version this will take about six minutes). *In order to make a summary, you will be making a note of the most important things that happen in the chapter.* Listen to the first significant event in the story and pause the CD-ROM. Model the writing of notes for the event on the display paper (see Resource Page F).

- Restart the CD-ROM and invite the class to take their own notes.

- Compare your notes with those of the class at the end of the chapter, as you add to the display.

- *What is the main purpose of the first chapter?* Answers might include:

> Introduces the narrator (Jim Hawkins) who will be one of the adventurers.
>
> Introduces the old sailor (Billy Bones), thereby giving a clue that the adversaries will be pirates.
>
> Gives clues that the adventure will concern buried treasure (sea chest – what does it contain?)
>
> Introduces Dr Livesey as one of the group of gentlemen who will seek the treasure.

- Refer back to the class checklist from the previous lesson. *Which points will be needed in writing a summary of chapter 1?*

- Model using your notes to write the summary (see Resource Page G).

- Point out how you have linked two or three of your notes in the same sentence:
  - this moves the summary along
  - uses fewer words than writing a sentence for each of the main points
  - keeps the summary to the point.

Independent, pair or guided work

- In pairs, the children orally rehearse possible opening sentences. Write a few of these on the board.

- The children use their own notes or yours to write their own summary of chapter 1.

- Remind the children to continually review their work and reread their sentences (aloud) to make sure the writing flows and makes sense.

Plenary

- With a response partner, the children read each other's summaries. Using Post-it™ notes, each writes a positive point and suggests a way to improve something else.

Planning Frames

Objective

We will analyse the plan for *Treasure Island* and another quest story

You need: Resource Pages E, H and I; another quest story with which the children are familiar (an infant book will be quick to read, simple to remember and will provide a plot that is easy to analyse, e.g. *Billy's Beetle*, by Mick Inkpen); OHTs (optional).

Whole class work

- Tell the children that they are going to use the structure of *Treasure Island* to plan their own story. They will analyse the plot and then analyse a simple quest story. (This planning format will be used to plan their own modern quest story in the next lesson. Over the following lessons they will fill in the details from their plan and at a later date will tell their story to the rest of the class.)

- Display and read through the second summary of *Treasure Island* (Resource Page E). Explain that this is a quest story – an adventure story where the main characters are trying to find something, in this case treasure. Looking for something is a very popular theme in fiction.

- *Can you think of any other quest stories?* For example, *The Hobbit, Cinderella, The Fellowship of the Ring* (this is a quest story in reverse – having inadvertently been given the treasure, Frodo's quest is to try to return it to its place of origin).

- Show a typical planning frame for a quest story (Resource Page H) – opening, build-up, dilemma, events, resolution, ending.

- Refer to the summary of *Treasure Island* and model how to analyse the story into its components to fit the planning grid. Show the children how to write simple notes into the framework (see Resource Page I). Remind them that this is not the place to write the story, just ideas for what happens next.

- Read aloud the chosen book for their own analysis.

Independent, pair or guided work

- Ask the children to use the planning framework to analyse the chosen story. One or two children could write a planning frame on an OHT so this could be displayed in the plenary.

Plenary

- Display transparencies and ask the children to explain their planning frame for class discussion. Reiterate the importance of having a resolution for each part of the dilemma.

Planning a Quest Story

Objective

We will plan the plot, characters and structure of our own quest story quickly and effectively

You need: Resource Pages H and I; whiteboards.

Whole class work

- Reread and discuss the planning frame for a quest story (Resource Page H). Review the completed frame for *Treasure Island* (Resource Page I) and the children's frames for the chosen class book from the previous lesson. Display Resource Page I for reference.

- *Today you will be planning a modern version of a quest story that you will use as a basis for developing a story to be told later.*

- The children use a whiteboard (or paper) to brainstorm three items that might be used as the subject of the quest. Each child selects one from their list and this is written on the board.

- On the display version of the planning frame, select one of the children's suggestions as the item that will be the object of the story.

- In pairs, the children think of three different settings where the chosen item could be located. Select an example from their suggestions and write this in the 'Build-up' section of the planning frame.

- Remind the children that *Treasure Island* is a novel and even in an abridged version on CD-Rom it takes over two and half hours to read aloud. Consequently they will need to simplify 'obstacles en route' and 'dilemmas' to just one or two.

- Explain that for every problem there must be a 'realistic' solution. Review possible scenarios:

  > can't find it ... can't get it ... get trapped ... get chased

- The children divide their whiteboards into two columns, headed *Problem* and *Solution*. The children work in pairs to write possible problems and solutions. Select one or two of their suggestions for your planning frame.

- Discuss the resolution and ending.

- Display your completed planning frame during independent work.

Independent, pair or guided work

- In pairs, the children plan their own quest story using the planning frame.

Plenary

- In pairs, the children tell each other briefly what their story will be about. The response partner comments on the interest level aroused.

Understanding Dialogue

Objectives

We will analyse how Stevenson uses dialogue. We will be able to contribute constructively to shared discussion about the book. We will also explore and annotate the features of dialogue

You need: Resource Pages J–N and EE; display paper for checklist.

Whole class work

- *Today's lesson will show how Stevenson uses dialogue and what purpose it serves in the story.*

- Display an OHT of Resource Page J and read the dialogues together. **Who is talking in each extract?**

- Using Resource Pages K and L, analyse the examples, mentioning how dialogue is set out: use of punctuation; purpose (for example, characterisation, to move story on); colloquialisms; contractions and interjections to make it sound realistic.

- *Using dialogue for characterisation should define the characters so thoroughly that if all the names were removed, the reader could still tell who was talking. It also gives the characters time to interact.*

- Explain that dialogue can also be used for other purposes too, for example:
  - Starting a story – it plunges the reader directly into the action or situation and creates a good hook.
  - Getting the reader asking questions and wanting to find out more.
  - Reporting in a few sentences an event that happened earlier.
  - Adding humour – a good way to show the personality of one of your characters.
  - Creating mood, for example, a character's dialogue can set the tone of urgency or danger.
  - Speeding up action with short passages of dialogue (and slowing down with longer ones).
  - Telling the reader when and where your story takes place. To be convincing dialogue must change to reflect when the story takes place, for example, "What's up?" (modern day,); "What takes your concern, my lord?" (medieval).

- *How would you know just by the dialogue that* Treasure Island *was set a long time ago?*

- Ask the children to remind you of what they have noted about dialogue from the shared reading and analysis. Start a class checklist (see checklist 2, Resource Page EE for ideas).

Independent, pair or guided work

- Read through the two additional extracts (Resource Pages M and N) and ensure that the children understand the language.

- The children analyse the dialogue, particularly noting the use of punctuation. They should work out why the author used dialogue at this point in the story.

Plenary

- For each of the items already noted on the checklist, ask the children to supply examples from the extracts.

- Feedback on the purpose of the dialogue.

Writing Dialogue

Objectives

We will find out how dialogue can be used effectively. We will rehearse dialogue between two characters, and learn how to set out dialogue with correct punctuation

You need: Resource Pages O, EE and FF; display paper.

Whole class work

- Explain that the purpose of this lesson is to learn how to write better dialogue.

- *Why do you think authors use dialogue in stories?* Write suggestions on the board.

- Review the class checklist for dialogue from the previous lesson.

- Display the OHT of two short dialogues that show mistakes often made in children's writing of speech (Resource Page O). Ask the children for their opinions and point out:
  - The speech is stilted.
  - No contractions have been used.
  - There are too many speech verbs such as 'replied', 'exclaimed'.
  - There are too many speech adverbs, for example, 'happily'.
  - In reality, we hardly ever say the name of the person we are talking to.
  - In the 2nd example the writer is using dialogue to explain rather than demonstrate, which diminishes the impact.

- Now model writing how to improve the dialogue (see example 4, Resource Page FF).

- *Authors base their characters on real or fictional people. They can imagine what X would have said in this situation. Words will be different depending on who's saying them, even if they are giving exactly the same information. Try and hear your character's voice in your head. For example, how would Mr Spock say he was angry compared with Long John Silver? Spock is a scientist: he's logical and his language is very precise. Long John Silver is a cunning pirate, more prone to defamations and exclamations such as "Shiver me timbers!"*

- Start a class checklist for writing dialogue (see checklist 3, Resource Page EE for ideas).

Independent, pair or guided work

- The children work in small groups. Select two children in each group to role play the meeting of two pirates. One is very nervous about meeting the other, but can't escape. This can be based on the conversation between Billy Bones and Black Dog from the previous lesson. The conversation will consist of about three interactions each. The children run through the dialogue two or three times, keeping as close to the original as possible. The rest of the group listen carefully.

- Using what they have heard as the starting point, the children write the dialogue between the two pirates.

Plenary

- Go through the items on the two checklists. Ask the children to underline the points they have included as each one is mentioned.

The Narrator

Objectives

We will find out more about the role of the narrator in a story, and why more than one narrator may be necessary. We will also present an extract from *Treasure Island* from a different point of view

You need: Resource Pages P and Q.

Whole class work

- *This purpose of this lesson is to find out more about how Stevenson uses narrators to tell his story.*

- Read together the extracts from chapters 12 and 16 (Resource Page P). Explain who the narrator is in each extract and what information can be learnt from the text.

- Ensure the children understand why Stevenson changed narrators. Explain that if Stevenson wanted to keep only one narrator, Jim would have had to report what went on through someone else's eyes, for example:

> "Later I was to learn from Dr Livesey what had gone on while I was on the island."

- Point out that writing from the viewpoint of a particular character is like the camera position chosen by a film director.

- *Writing in the first person helps the reader to respond to the character but limits the amount of information as it depends on what the narrator sees.*

- Read through the extract from chapter 15 where Jim sees Ben Gunn for the first time (Resource Page Q).

Independent, pair or guided work

- Give the children a few minutes to prepare their ideas about the arrival of the *Hispaniola* at the island from Ben Gunn's point of view.

- *What would he have been thinking after spending three years alone on the island? Did his thoughts change as he saw pirates he knew approaching? What did he think of his first meeting with Jim?*

- Select a child to hot seat the part of Ben Gunn. The others ask questions about Ben's views of the arrival of the *Hispaniola*. The activity can then be repeated in groups with the children taking turns to role play Ben.

Plenary

- *How would having Long John Silver as the narrator affect the story?*

- Ensure that the children understand:
  - a first person narrator will be central to the plot
  - readers respond to what the narrator experiences
  - a first person narrator can only tell what they see or experience
  - a first person narrator has to report through others' eyes or through flashback anything else going on in the plot.

Different Viewpoints

Objective

We will write an extract from two viewpoints

You need: Resource Page R.

Whole class work	• Review how Stevenson uses two narrators in *Treasure Island*. Emphasise that when writing from a first person narrator's viewpoint, it is necessary to keep rereading to check for consistency. It is very easy to slip into third person narration.
	• *Today I am going to show you how to write from the perspective of another narrator.*
	• Reread the first section of chapter 4 to the part where Jim and his mother return to the inn alone.
	• Model writing as a neighbour from the hamlet where Jim and Mrs Hawkins ask for help (Resource Page R).
	• Mention the importance of standing in the narrator's shoes, and explain that different people will see the same event differently. Jack reports as though he and his mother were left on their own to sort out the problem themselves. In your modelled alternative, the neighbour could say that lots of help was offered but refused.
Independent, pair or guided work	• Remind the children of their role play from the previous lesson.
	• Split the class into two groups. Group 1 write an extract from Ben Gunn's viewpoint when he sees the *Hispaniola* and Long John Silver for the first time after being marooned.
	• The other group write the extract from Silver's viewpoint when he sees the island and wonders whether Ben Gunn is still marooned on it.
	• Emphasise the importance of putting themselves into the character's shoes and writing what the character would be thinking and doing.
Plenary	• Pair up the children, one each from the two groups. Choose one or two pairs, listen to their extracts and ask the class to discuss the effectiveness of their writing, what works well and why.

Dilemma and Resolution

Objectives

We will analyse how Stevenson resolved the dilemmas in *Treasure Island*. We will also collect phrases or linking words to move a dilemma to its resolution

You need: Resource Pages I and S–V; display paper.

Whole class work

● Remind the children that Stevenson has written many dilemmas in the book. ***What are the dilemmas that Jim has to solve?*** (Refer back to the planning frame, Resource Page I.)

● ***Today we are going to look at how Stevenson moves from a dilemma to a resolution. We will examine how he builds the tension and the phrases he uses to move from the dilemma to the resolution.***

● Read the extract from chapter 33 (Resource Page S). Using the example analysis (Resource Page T), identify the build-up in tension and the move to the resolution.

● Start a class collection of useful phrases with 'But just then …' (to be completed later in the lesson, see below).

Independent, pair or guided work

● Give out further extracts for the children to analyse (Resource Page U). Ask the children to read the dilemmas from the story. In each case, the children identify the resolution and any words or phrases used by Stevenson to move from one to the other. These can be recorded on the planning frame (Resource Page V).

● Some children may have time to look through books with which they are familiar to find any other linking phrases.

Plenary

● Ask the children to identify the words that Stevenson (and other authors) uses to move from dilemma to resolution. Add these to the planning frame.

● ***What other words or phrases might be useful?***

> quite suddenly … straight after that … no sooner had he … what seemed like a lifetime after …
> in no time at all … at that moment

● The children can practise using their phrase in an appropriate sentence.

Features of Stevenson's Style

Objectives

We will become familiar with the writing style of Robert Louis Stevenson as a classic author. We will learn how to select similar sentence structure to imitate the style in our own writing. We will consider word choice and the use of semi-colons

You need: Resource Pages W–Y and FF; display paper for a checklist.

Whole class work

- *Today we will look at the first and last paragraphs of the book for features that Stevenson used in his style of writing. You will then write an alternative ending, in Stevenson's style.*

- Read the two extracts on Resource Page W. *Are there any striking features that you notice immediately?*

- Annotate the first paragraph (see Resource Page X), noting in particular:
  - the length of the sentences
  - the use of words no longer in common use
  - the structure of the sentences
  - the proliferation of commas and semi-colons.

- Read the last paragraph and scribe the children's analysis of the style on to the display paper.

- Ask a child to write the features as they are noted on to a class checklist (see checklist 5, Resource Page FF for ideas).

- Model writing the start of a new final paragraph (see Resource Page Y). Identify the features of Stevenson's style as you model the writing.

- Ask the children for ideas about what happens next.

Independent, pair or guided work

- The children can either conclude the new ending (begun in whole class work) or write their own ending. Remind the children they are trying to write in the style of Stevenson. Display the class checklist.

Plenary

- In pairs, the children swap books and read each other's work. They write a response to the work which should praise any features included from the checklist and offer suggestions as to how to improve the writing further.

Film Reviews

Objectives

We will investigate features of film reviews. Using information from the comparison of film and book versions of *Treasure Island* and a planning frame to help plan effectively and quickly, we will write a review of the film of *Treasure Island*

You need: Resource Pages Z, AA and FF. The children will need to view the film before this lesson.

Whole class work

- *We are going to use our knowledge of the film* Treasure Island *to write a review.*

- *The purpose of a review is to give an opinion about a film. Unlike the book summary, this type of writing includes some facts, but most of the review is the opinion of the reviewer. Viewers should read several reviews to find out about films as reviewers' opinions differ.*

- Read the children the film review of *Shrek* and annotate it (Resource Page Z).

- Ask the children to point out the features from your analysis and scribe these on to a class checklist of features of a film review (see checklist 6, Resource Page FF for ideas).

- Model how to use the checklist to provide a planning frame to write another review, then model completing the frame in note form (Resource Page AA).

- Make references to ideas that arose from the comparison work in previous lessons, for example, the changed ending.

- Model taking the notes from the first section ('Hook the reader'), to write an opening sentence:

> All aboard, me hearties, for this tale of swashbuckling pirates and buried treasure – a classic adaptation of Stevenson's <u>Treasure Island</u>; not to be missed on a wet, cold Sunday afternoon.

Independent, pair or guided work

- The children complete the review from the notes. Some children may be encouraged to write their own opening sentence as well.

Plenary

- Hide the checklist and remove the planning frame.

- Ask a child to read a sentence from their review and tell you the feature that the sentence demonstrates. Scribe the feature on the board.

- Continue until the children think all features are present.

- Display the checklist and check the new list against it.

Narrative into Playscript

Objectives

We will read and review a synopsis of finding the treasure (end of chapter 32, start of chapter 33). We will learn how to make decisions as a playwright. Then we will improvise speech in order to act out the scene

You need: Resource Pages BB, CC and FF.

Whole class work

- *In order to present* Treasure Island *as a film, it has to be turned from a narrative into a film script.*

- *Films give a vast amount of visual information, so that the dialogue can be quite sparse in comparison. Producing* Treasure Island *as a play may require more dialogue in comparison, because the visual information will be more limited.*

- Explain that in the next three lessons, the children will take an extract from *Treasure Island* and rewrite and act it as a play.

- Read the synopsis of the climax of the book, when the pirates find the empty treasure chest (Resource Page BB).

- Ask the children for ideas to make a class checklist of the features of plays (see checklist 7, Resource Page FF for ideas).

- Explain that their first task as writer of the play is to decide upon the stage instructions (setting), the characters, and which parts of the scene will be shown through actions (stage directions) and which through speech.

- Model making these decisions using the first paragraph of the text (see Resource Page CC).

Independent, pair or guided work

- Read through the other two paragraphs. Tell the class to imagine the scene starts at paragraph two.

- In groups of at least three (LJS, Jim and George), the children make decisions about the setting of the scene, characters required, stage directions. Then they analyse which parts of the text should be speech and which could be shown through actions.

- From the guidelines decided by the group, the children act out the scene improvising the speech.

Plenary

- The children watch one group's improvisation work and comment critically.

- *As a member of an audience, does it entertain you? What parts are too drawn out? Which parts work well? Why? What could the group do to improve the work?*

Writing a Playscript

Objective

We will identify what changes are needed to transform a narrative into a playscript

You need: Resource Page BB–DD.

Whole class work

- *Today we will continue looking at how to transform a narrative into a playscript.*

- Read the first paragraph of the synopsis again (Resource Page BB). Using notes from the previous lesson (Resource Page CC), model how to change the text from a narrative into a playscript (Resource Page DD).

- While working, continue to add features to the class checklist of play features from the previous lesson.

Independent, pair or guided work

- In groups, the children act out the remaining two paragraphs of the synopsis.

- The children use three different coloured highlighters to identify narrative that will need to be written as stage instructions (setting the scene) or stage directions (describing actions or how something is said), and which parts can be turned into dialogue.

Plenary

- Discuss how the scene has to change slightly when written as a playscript rather than a narrative.

- The children should identify descriptions changed into stage instructions and directions, the need to add dialogue to tell the audience what is happening, and that some parts of the narrative may be omitted, for example:

> Silver now behaves in a friendly manner towards Jim, a stark change from his early antagonistic behaviour.

could be condensed to:

> LJS: (friendly)

66

(Pupil copymaster)

Web site summary

Robert Louis Stevenson wrote *Treasure Island* in 1881. It is set in the days of sailing ships and pirates and tells of the adventures of Jim Hawkins and his search for the buried treasure of an evil pirate, Captain Flint.

The story begins at 'The Admiral Benbow', the inn that belongs to Jim Hawkins' parents. A mysterious stranger called Billy Bones, who rents a room at the inn, warns Jim to keep a lookout for a 'one-legged man'. One day, Billy is visited by a beggar called 'Blind Pew' who gives him the 'black spot' which is the mark of imminent death among pirate crews. After Blind Pew leaves, Billy collapses and dies.

Jim finds a map in Billy's sea chest just before Blind Pew returns with a band of evil pirates. Jim and his mother quickly hide before the pirates ransack the Inn looking for the map. Suddenly soldiers arrive and the pirates escape, except for Blind Pew who is accidentally trampled to death by the soldiers' horses.

Jim takes the map to Squire Trelawney and Doctor Livesey who realise that it shows where Captain Flint, an evil and heartless pirate, has buried his stolen treasure. The Squire and the Doctor decide to go and find the treasure and invite Jim to come along. The Squire then buys a ship called the *Hispaniola* and hires a crew led by the respected Captain Smollet. The ship's cook is a one-legged man called Long John Silver whom everyone admires.

The ship sets sail and Captain Smollet immediately begins to doubt the trustworthiness of his crew. However, the night before they reach Treasure Island Jim overhears Silver and other members of the crew plotting to kill them all. He realises that Long John Silver and most of the crew are actually pirates and were once members of Captain Flint's crew.

Jim warns the Doctor, the Squire and the Captain about the crew's evil plans. The Captain sends most of the pirates ashore and Jim decides, at the last moment, to go ashore with them. Once there, he hides in the woods.

While Jim is hiding he comes across Ben Gunn, an ex-pirate who had been marooned on the island three years ago, by his crewmates. Ben has given up piracy and promises to help Jim and his friends. Meanwhile the Captain and the others abandon the *Hispaniola* and take refuge in an old stockade on the Island.

The pirates quickly realise that their plans have been discovered and attack the Captain and the others to get the treasure map. However, for the time being the Captain and his crew are safe in the stockade.

Jim manages to sneak into the stockade and is reunited with his friends. They spend the night in the stockade and the next morning Silver approaches waving a flag of truce. Silver offers them their lives in exchange for the treasure map but the Captain refuses and soon another gunfight starts. The stockade is attacked by the pirates, who are fought off, though there are men killed on both sides. Captain Smollett is also injured.

adapted from **http://www.ukoln.ac.uk/services/treasure**

Web site summary (continued)

Jim decides to escape from the stockade and goes off without telling the others. He finds a boat that Ben Gunn has told him he has hidden and then sails out to the *Hispaniola* and cuts its mooring ropes. He falls asleep in the boat exhausted.

In the morning he only just manages to escape from drowning as the sea has become very rough. Luckily he spots the drifting *Hispaniola* and manages to board her. There are only two pirates on board, one of whom has been killed in a drunken brawl by the other. After a terrifying fight, Jim kills the last pirate and manages to steer the ship into a small cove. He then heads back to the stockade to rejoin his friends.

The stockade is now in the hands of Long John Silver and his mates. Jim is captured and is given the choice to join them. When he refuses the pirates want to kill him but Silver talks them out of it. Silver tells Jim that the Doctor has given him the map and also abandons the stockade in exchange for being allowed to go free.

Silver tells Jim that he is now on the side of the Doctor. At this point the pirates attempt to give Silver the black spot but withdraw it when he reveals that he has the map. They agree to go and find the treasure the next day.

The treasure hunt begins and Jim is dragged along. The weather is hot and sweaty and the pirates are edgy. When they finally reach the spot where the treasure should have been hidden they discover only an empty chest!

Silver immediately realises that there will be trouble and gives Jim a pistol with which to defend himself. The pirates turn angrily on Silver and are just about to attack him when there is a shot from the woods that kills one of them. The Doctor and Ben Gunn then appear and the pirates run off, heading for the remaining long boat left from the *Hispaniola*.

Jim and his friends get there first and demolish the boat. At this point Ben Gunn reveals that he had dug up the treasure several years ago and it is now in his cave. Jim takes everyone to the *Hispaniola* and they transport the treasure from Ben's cave to her hold. Silver still claims to be on the Doctor's side and helps them at every opportunity. Finally they set sail and leave Treasure Island and the last couple of pirates behind. They first sail the *Hispaniola* to America to get more crewmen and moor there for one night.

In the morning they discover that Silver and some of the treasure have disappeared. Finally they return home, the Captain makes a full recovery, Ben Gunn becomes a respectable citizen and Jim swears never to go chasing treasure again. No one ever hears of Long John Silver again.

adapted from **http://www.ukoln.ac.uk/services/treasure**

(Exemplar analysis)

Example of analysis of web site summary

Author identified in first sentence. First paragraph sums up main idea of book.

Chronological order, present tense.

Gives main details only.

Many varied connectives to move story along (examples underlined).

Summary reports what happens without the need to build suspense.

Many examples of compound sentences: two main clauses linked by 'and'.

Detail of chapter is reduced to one or two main points.

Opening: task to find something – finds pirate map and decides to seek the treasure.

Establish setting: on board the Hispaniola and on Treasure Island.

Characters set off and overcome obstacles en route. Jim discovers the plot and tells Captain.

Complex sentence: main and subordinate clause.

Robert Louis Stevenson wrote *Treasure Island* in 1881. It is set in the days of sailing ships and pirates and tells of the adventures of Jim Hawkins and his search for the buried treasure of an evil pirate, Captain Flint.

The story begins at 'The Admiral Benbow', the inn that belongs to Jim Hawkins' parents. A mysterious stranger called Billy Bones, who rents a room at the inn, warns Jim to keep a lookout for a 'one-legged man'. One day, Billy is visited by a beggar called 'Blind Pew' who gives him the 'black spot' which is the mark of imminent death among pirate crews. After Blind Pew leaves, Billy collapses and dies.

Jim finds a map in Billy's sea chest just before Blind Pew returns with a band of evil pirates. Jim and his mother quickly hide before the pirates ransack the Inn looking for the map. Suddenly soldiers arrive and the pirates escape, except for Blind Pew who is accidentally trampled to death by the soldiers' horses.

Jim takes the map to Squire Trelawney and Doctor Livesey who realise that it shows where Captain Flint, an evil and heartless pirate, has buried his stolen treasure. The Squire and the Doctor decide to go and find the treasure and invite Jim to come along. The Squire then buys a ship called the *Hispaniola* and hires a crew led by the respected Captain Smollet. The ship's cook is a one-legged man called Long John Silver whom everyone admires.

The ship sets sail and Captain Smollet immediately begins to doubt the trustworthiness of his crew. However, the night before they reach Treasure Island Jim overhears Silver and other members of the crew plotting to kill them all. He realises that Long John Silver and most of the crew are actually pirates and were once members of Captain Flint's crew.

Jim warns the Doctor, the Squire and the Captain about the crew's evil plans. The Captain sends most of the pirates ashore and Jim decides, at the last moment, to go ashore with them. Once there, he hides in the woods.

While Jim is hiding he comes across Ben Gunn, an ex-pirate who had been marooned on the island three years ago, by his crewmates. Ben has given up piracy and promises to help Jim and his friends. Meanwhile the Captain and the others abandon the *Hispaniola* and take refuge in an old stockade on the Island.

The pirates quickly realise that their plans have been discovered and attack the Captain and the others to get the treasure map. However, for the time being the Captain and his crew are safe in the stockade.

Jim manages to sneak into the stockade and is reunited with his friends. They spend the night in the stockade and the next morning Silver approaches waving a flag of truce. Silver offers them their lives in exchange for the treasure map but the Captain refuses and soon another gunfight starts. The stockade is attacked by the pirates, who are fought off, though there are men killed on both sides. Captain Smollett is also injured.

adapted from **http://www.ukoln.ac.uk/services/treasure**

(Exemplar analysis)

Example of analysis of summary (continued)

Dilemma: trapped in stockade, little food. Events: escapes.

Jim decides to escape from the stockade and goes off without telling the others. He finds a boat that Ben Gunn has told him he has hidden and then sails out to the *Hispaniola* and cuts its mooring ropes. He falls asleep in the boat exhausted.

In the morning he only just manages to escape from drowning as the sea has become very rough. Luckily he spots the drifting *Hispaniola* and manages to board her. There are only two pirates on board, one of whom has been killed in a drunken brawl by the other. After a terrifying fight, Jim kills the last pirate and manages to steer the ship into a small cove. He then heads back to the stockade to rejoin his friends.

Dilemma: gets trapped at sea. Events: rescues himself, kills pirate, ensures Hispaniola is in safe place for his return with treasure.

Dilemma: gets caught Events: LJS saves him from other pirates.

The stockade is now in the hands of Long John Silver and his mates. Jim is captured and is given the choice to join them. When he refuses the pirates want to kill him but Silver talks them out of it. Silver tells Jim that the Doctor has given him the map and also abandons the stockade in exchange for being allowed to go free.

Silver tells Jim that he is now on the side of the Doctor. At this point the pirates attempt to give Silver the black spot but withdraw it when he reveals that he has the map. They agree to go and find the treasure the next day.

Dilemma: pirates also trapped by LJS. Events: go along with him because he has map.

Events: no treasure in chest.

The treasure hunt begins and Jim is dragged along. The weather is hot and sweaty and the pirates are edgy. When they finally reach the spot where the treasure should have been hidden they discover only an empty chest!

Silver immediately realises that there will be trouble and gives Jim a pistol with which to defend himself. The pirates turn angrily on Silver and are just about to attack him when there is a shot from the woods that kills one of them. The Doctor and Ben Gunn then appear and the pirates run off, heading for the remaining long boat left from the *Hispaniola*.

Events: help arrives to support LJS and Jim.

Resolution: treasure found and start journey home.

Jim and his friends get there first and demolish the boat. At this point Ben Gunn reveals that he had dug up the treasure several years ago and it is now in his cave. Jim takes everyone to the *Hispaniola* and they transport the treasure from Ben's cave to her hold. Silver still claims to be on the Doctor's side and helps them at every opportunity. Finally they set sail and leave Treasure Island and the last couple of pirates behind. They first sail the *Hispaniola* to America to get more crewmen and moor there for one night.

Connectives used to draw the summary to a conclusion.

In the morning they discover that Silver and some of the treasure have disappeared. Finally they return home, the Captain makes a full recovery, Ben Gunn becomes a respectable citizen and Jim swears never to go chasing treasure again. No one ever hears of Long John Silver again.

Ending – the final comment.

Resolution continued: what happened to main characters.

adapted from **http://www.ukoln.ac.uk/services/treasure**

Summary only includes what actually happens in the story, not opinions and feelings of the reader as might be seen in a book review.

Classworks Literacy Year 6 © Paula Ross, Nelson Thornes Ltd 2003

70

(Pupil copymaster)

An alternative summary

Stevenson's most famous novel and enduringly popular adventure story, *Treasure Island* was published in 1883.

The story starts when an old, scarred sailor arrives at the Admiral Benbow inn, where young Jim Hawkins works. Billy Bones, as the man is known, fills Jim's ears with stories of the open sea and warns him to be on the lookout for a one-legged man. Later, some of Bones' former pirate shipmates appear and give him a slip of paper with a black spot on it, terrifying the old man. Bones dies of a stroke, and Jim escapes with his treasure map as the other pirates scour the Inn. Jim takes the map to Dr. Livesey, who forms a plan with his friend Squire Trelawney to sail after the treasure, which was buried by the pirate Captain Flint.

Jim travels to Bristol to meet up with the ship, the *Hispaniola*. In Bristol, he meets the ship's cook, Long John Silver, a one-legged man who recommends many of the ship's crew to Trelawney. Despite Billy Bones warning about a one-legged man, Jim is won over by Silver's friendly charm. Then, after an uneventful voyage, Jim is on deck one night and overhears Silver plotting a mutiny. Soon after, land is sighted, and Jim tells the Captain, Livesey and Trelawney what he's heard. Alarmed, the men plan to split up the crew to improve their odds, and Jim goes ashore with Silver and the others. While on the island, Jim sees Silver kill a sailor who won't join the mutiny and meets Ben Gunn, a marooned sailor who lives on the island. Meanwhile, Dr Livesey, Squire Trelawney and the others leave the ship and find a stockade on the island, where they settle in for a fight.

Under Captain Smollett's command, they weather the pirates' first attack. Jim arrives at the stockade and joins the defenders. Long John Silver comes to negotiate with them, but the captain sends him away. The pirates storm the stockade, and several men are killed and Captain Smollett wounded in a bloody battle.

The next day, Jim sneaks away with a plan to cut loose the *Hispaniola* and strand the pirates. After a dangerous trip, Jim succeeds in freeing the ship. He then jumps aboard, where he finds one watchman dead and the other drunk and wounded. Jim and the wounded pirate team up to steer the ship; then the pirate turns on Jim, but Jim kills the pirate in the ensuing fight.

After anchoring the ship in a new place to fool the pirates, Jim returns to the stockade, where he is captured by Silver's men. Silver tells Jim that Dr Livesey and the others agreed to give the pirates the stockade and the treasure map. (Dr Livesey did this because he discovered that Ben Gunn had already dug up the treasure.) Silver lets Jim live when Jim promises to testify for him if the mutineers are caught. Silver's men are losing confidence in him, and Silver's treatment of Jim makes them suspicious.

The pirates set out to look for the treasure, but find only an empty hole. When they turn on Silver and Jim, Dr Livesey, Ben Gunn and another loyal man ambush the pirates and drive them off. They rejoin the Captain and Squire Trelawney, who are waiting with the treasure.

They sail back to England, but Silver escapes when they land in South America.

(Exemplar material)

Example of modelling note-taking for a summary

Chapter 1, The Old Sea-Dog at the 'Admiral Benbow'

Write this on the board ...	... while you are saying this
1 Jim's father kept an inn	*Title of chapter includes Admiral Benbow so no need to write it again.*
2 Arrival of scarred sailor	*Point out that there is a lot of description about the sailor but there is no need to include all of it here – writing 'scarred' will jog my memory about the rest or I can find it again from the text.*
3 Sailor pleased that few people came to the inn	*One reason why he stayed at the inn.*
4 Looking out for one-legged man	*Mention of another possible character.*
5 Often drunk	*Important characteristic.*
6 Told stories, father thought put off customers	*Wants to keep people away from the inn?*
7 Stayed many months without paying	*Important characteristic – nobody dare ask him.*
8 Dr Livesey only one to stand up to him	*Mention of another named character.*

(Exemplar material)

Example of modelling a summary from notes

Chapter 1, The Old Sea-Dog at the 'Admiral Benbow'

Write this on the board ...	... while you are saying this
	Get Notes 1 and 2 into the first sentence to introduce as many characters as possible.
Jim Hawkins, the narrator,	*Function of commas to introduce, separate and enclose. Here commas used to enclose the narrator because Jim Hawkins and the narrator are the same person.*
describes	*Present tense.*
the arrival one day of a scarred, old sailor (Billy Bones)	*Use brackets to put in extra information.*
at the Admiral Benbow, an inn run by Jim's mother and ailing father.	*Add an extra clause to explain what the Admiral Benbow is and to introduce two other characters. Next sentence add the important fact that he didn't want to be found (Note 3)*
The sailor is looking for lodging at an out-of-the-way inn, and seems to want to avoid other sailors.	*Reread and decide that this is an ideal place to add a further description of the sailor. Explain that you are going to put in a subordinate clause about his sea chest – where Jim will eventually find the treasure map so therefore vital to the story.*
The sailor, who has nothing with him but his worn clothing and a large sea-chest,	*The use of commas to enclose the subordinate clause.*
is looking for lodging at an out-of-the-way inn, and seems to want to avoid other sailors.	*Now add Note 4.*
Later, he tells Jim to be especially on the lookout for a one-legged sailor.	*Conclude the summary with Notes 5, 6 and 7 in one sentence.*
The old sailor stays	*Continue to use present tense.*
for months	*Note 7.*
and begins to terrorize Jim's family and the inn's guests with his loud demands	*Note 6.*
and violent, drunken behaviour.	*Note 5.*
At the end of the chapter one person dares to confront the old sailor – Dr Livesey, the town physician.	*Use of 'old' language.*

Classworks Literacy Year 6 © Paula Ross, Nelson Thornes Ltd 2003

Planning frame for a quest story

Opening	Build-up	Dilemma	Events	Resolution and ending
Task established to find something	Establish the setting Characters set off and overcome obstacles en route	Options: ● Can't find it ● Can't get in ● Get trapped ● Get chased	Struggle and overcome each problem	Arriive back at the start, task accomplished Final comment

(Exemplar material)

Planning frame for a quest story (*Treasure Island*)

(Format for the quest story from Year 6 exemplification planning booklet)

Opening	Build-up	Dilemma	Events	Resolution and ending
Task established to find something	Establish the setting Characters set off and overcome obstacles en route	Options: ● Can't find it ● Can't get in ● Get trapped ● Get chased	Struggle and overcome each problem	Arrive back at the start, task accomplished Final comment
Finds a pirate's map and decides to seek the treasure	On board the *Hispaniola* and at Treasure Island Jim discovers the plot and *tells Captain*	Blind Pew and pirates searching for Jim because he has the map Gets trapped at sea Gets caught by pirates No treasure in the chest	Help arrives and pirates scatter. Blind Pew is killed Saves himself and kills pirate, checks *Hispaniola* is in a safe place for his return with treasure Long John Silver saves him from other pirates Help arrives to support Long John Silver and Jim	Treasure found and start journey home Explain what happens to the Captain, Ben Gunn, Silver and Jim The final comment: *No one ever hears of Long John Silver again*

Some dialogue to read and analyse

Dialogue (1)

"Well then," said he, "this is the berth for me. Here you are, matey," he cried to the man who trundled the barrow; "bring up alongside and help up my chest. I'll stay here a bit," he continued. "I'm a plain man; rum and bacon and eggs is what I want, and that head up there for to watch ships off. What you mought call me? You mought call me captain. Oh I see what you're at there;" and he threw down three or four gold pieces on the threshold. "You can tell me when I've worked through that," says he, looking as fierce as a commander.

Dialogue (2)

"But look here," he went on, "here's what I want to know, Barbecue: how long are we a-going to stand off and on like a blessed bumboat? I've had a'most enough o' Cap'n Smollett; he's hazed me long enough, by thunder! I want to go into that cabin, I do. I want their pickles and wines, and that."

"Israel," said Silver, "your head ain't much account, nor ever was. But you're able to hear, I reckon; leastways, your ears is big enough. Now, here's what I say: you'll berth forward, and you'll live hard, and you'll speak soft, and you'll keep sober till I give the word; and you may lay to that, my son."

(Exemplar analysis)

Example of analysis of dialogue (1)

Extract from chapter 1, the arrival of Bones at the Admiral Benbow — example of a monologue (speech by one person, usually lengthy) — purpose to introduce and develop a new character.

A pause. Point out use of speech marks, need for punctuation at end of phrase or clause before final speech marks. Need to close and reopen speech marks when the sentence is broken. No need for speech marks at full stop if same person continues to speak.

Clues that the character is a seaman (examples in italics).

New speaker, new paragraph.

Spelling of 'might' to show spoken accent, gives an indication of where he could be from and that he is probably not a well-educated man.

Short for headland.

"Well then," said he, "this is the *berth* for me. Here you are, <u>matey</u>," he cried to the man who trundled the barrow; "bring up *alongside* and help up my *chest*. <u>I'll</u> stay here a bit," he continued. "I'm a plain man; *rum* and bacon and eggs is what I want, and that *head* up there for to *watch ships* off. What you mought call me? You mought call me *captain*. Oh I see what <u>you're</u> at there;" and he threw down three or four gold pieces on the threshold. "You can tell me when <u>I've</u> worked through that," says he, looking as fierce as a commander.

Other indicators to his character.

People naturally use colloquialisms and contractions in speech (examples underlined).

(Exemplar analysis)

Example of analysis of dialogue (2)

Extract from chapter 11, Jim overhears the pirates while he is hiding in the apple cask – example of dialogue (conversation between two or more characters) – purpose to show what the author wants to tell the reader. Instead of using narration the characters demonstrate through their interaction. Also allows characterisation to develop.

Nickname of Long John Silver as he had been a ship's cook. Barbecue from French word *boucan* meaning to grill meat, also the term from which 'buccaneers' came – pirates based in the West Indies.

Contractions and use of 'pirate' language.

Small boat used to peddle provisions and wares to ships anchored offshore.

New speaker, new paragraph.

"But look here," he went on, "here's what I want to know, Barbecue: how long are we a-going to stand off and on like a blessed bumboat? I've had a'most enough o' Cap'n Smollett; he's hazed me long enough, by thunder! I want to go into that cabin, I do. I want their pickles and wines, and that."

"Israel," said Silver, "your head ain't much account, nor ever was. But you're able to hear, I reckon; leastways, your ears is big enough. Now, here's what I say: you'll berth forward, and you'll live hard, and you'll speak soft, and you'll keep sober till I give the word; and you may lay to that, my son."

Dialogue shows some of the pirates are getting impatient to take over the ship while Long John Silver, their leader, is telling them they will do as he says until he gives word.

LJS insults Israel, the coxswain, to show he is in charge.

Dialogue for you to annotate (1)

Dialogue between Captain Smollett and Mr Trelawney, the Squire, after Jim Hawkins has told them what he overheard from the apple cask.

"You, sir, are the captain. It is for you to speak," says Mr. Trelawney grandly.

"First point," began Mr. Smollett. "We must go on, because we can't turn back. If I gave the word to go about, they would rise at once. Second point, we have time before us - at least until this treasure's found. Third point, there are faithful hands. Now, sir, it's got to come to blows sooner or later, and what I propose is to take time by the forelock, as the saying is, and come to blows some fine day when they least expect it. We can count, I take it, on your own home servants, Mr Trelawney?"

"As upon myself," declared the squire.

"Three," reckoned the captain; "ourselves make seven, counting Hawkins here. Now, about the honest hands?"

Dialogue for you to annotate (2)

"Come, Bill, you know me; you know an old shipmate, Bill, surely," said the stranger. The captain made a sort of gasp.

"Black Dog!" said he.

"And who else?" returned the other, getting more at his ease. "Black Dog as ever was, come for to see his old shipmate Billy, at the Admiral Benbow inn. Ah, Bill, Bill, we have seen a sight of times, us two, since I lost them two talons," holding up his mutilated hand.

"Now, look here," said the captain; "you've run me down; here I am; well, then, speak up; what is it?"

"That's you, Bill," returned Black Dog, "you're in the right of it, Billy. I'll have a glass of rum from this dear child here, as I've took such a liking to; and we'll sit down, if you please, and talk square, like old shipmates."

How successful are these examples of dialogue?

"Hello, how are you, Jim?" said Long John Silver cheerfully.

"I am fine. How are you, Long John Silver?" replied Jim spiritedly.

"I am well. And how are the captain and the Squire?" whispered Long John Silver excitedly.

"They are fine. What about the hands?" answered Jim distractedly.

"Why, I believe you are angry."
"Yes, I am. I am very angry."

Classworks Literacy Year 6 © Paula Ross, Nelson Thornes Ltd 2003

(Pupil copymaster)

Extracts from chapters 12 and 16

Extract from chapter 12, Council of War

> I was surprised at the coolness with which John avowed his knowledge of the island, and I own I was half-frightened when I saw him drawing nearer to myself. He did not know, to be sure, that I had overheard his council from the apple barrel, and yet I had by this time taken such a horror of his cruelty, duplicity, and power that I could scarce conceal a shudder when he laid his hand upon my arm.
>
> "Ah," says he, "this here is a sweet spot, this island – a sweet spot for a lad to get ashore on. You'll bathe, and you'll climb trees, and you'll hunt goats, you will; and you'll get aloft on them hills like a goat yourself. Why, it makes me young again. I was going to forget my timber leg, I was. It's a pleasant thing to be young and have ten toes, and you may lay to that. When you want to go a bit of exploring, you just ask old John, and he'll put up a snack for you to take along."
>
> And clapping me in the friendliest way upon the shoulder, he hobbled off forward and went below.
>
> *The narrator of most of the story is Jim Hawkins. When Jim is narrating, the reader receives his thoughts, feelings and opinions. Here he is trying to conceal his anger and hatred at Long John Silver's touch on this arm, when he has just heard Silver plotting to kill the Captain and the other honest men. Stevenson is writing through a first person narrator. Using a first person narrator adds to the suspense of the story as the reader is only getting one person's view of the events.*

Extract from chapter 16, How the Ship was Abandoned

> It was about half past one – three bells in the sea phrase – that the two boats went ashore from the *Hispaniola*. The Captain, the Squire, and I were talking matters over in the cabin. Had there been a breath of wind, we should have fallen on the six mutineers who were left aboard with us, slipped our cable, and away to sea. But the wind was wanting; and to complete our helplessness, down came Hunter with the news that Jim Hawkins had slipped into a boat and was gone ashore with the rest.
>
> *Here, Dr Livesey has taken over as narrator. This is because Stevenson has sent Jim off to the island with the pirates and so Jim can't tell the reader what is happening on board ship. Dr Livesey continues as narrator for three chapters (16, 17 and 18), then the narration reverts to Jim. Stevenson is still writing with a first person narrator, even though there has been a change from Jim to Livesey.*

(**Pupil copymaster**)

Extract from chapter 15, The Man of the Island

From the side of the hill, which was here steep and stony, a spout of gravel was dislodged, and fell rattling and bounding through the trees. My eyes turned instinctively in the direction, and I saw a figure leap with great rapidity behind the trunk of a pine. What it was, whether bear or man or monkey, I could in no wise tell. It seemed dark and shaggy; more I knew not. But the terror of this new apparition brought me to a stand.

I was now, it seemed, cut off upon both sides; behind me the murderers, before me this lurking nondescript. And immediately I began to prefer the dangers that I knew to those I knew not. Silver himself appeared less terrible in contrast with this creature of the woods, and I turned on my heel, and looking sharply behind me over my shoulder, began to retract my steps in the direction of the boats.

Instantly the figure reappeared, and, making a wide circuit began to head me off. I was tired, at any rate; but had I been as fresh as when I rose, I could see it was in vain for me to contend in speed with such an adversary.

From trunk to trunk the creature flitted like a deer, running manlike on two legs but unlike any man that I had ever seen, stooping almost double as it ran. Yet a man it was, I could no longer be in doubt about that.

I began to recall what I had heard of cannibals. I was within an ace of calling for help. But the mere fact that he was man, however wild, had somewhat reassured me, and my fear of Silver began to revive in proportion. I stood still, therefore and cast about for some method of escape; and as I was so thinking, the recollection of my pistol flashed into my mind. As soon as I remembered I was not defenceless, courage glowed again in my heart; and I set my face resolutely for this man of the island, and walked briskly towards him.

He was concealed by this time behind another tree trunk, but he must have been watching me closely, for as soon as I began to move in his direction he reappeared and took a step to meet me. Then he hesitated, drew back, came forward again, and at last, to my wonder and confusion, threw himself on his knees and held out his clasped hands in supplication.

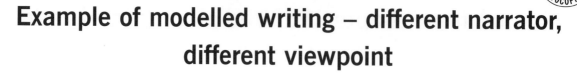

(Exemplar material)

Example of modelled writing – different narrator, different viewpoint

Write this on the board ...	... while you are saying this
Narrator: a neighbour from the hamlet Episode: Jim and Mrs Hawkins ask for help to see off Blind Pew and his followers	*I need to decide who the neighbour is: Jack Little, farm labourer in his 30s.*
There was such a banging upon my door, just as I	*Use of first person pronouns throughout.*
was rising from the fire to go to my bed. The recently bereaved	*Use information you already know to keep close to the original text.*
Mrs Hawkins and her young son Jim, out of breath and looking half scared to death, were standing on my doorstep.	*Point out the different sentence organisations in order to add variety to the writing.*
It soon became clear to me that there had been trouble up at the Admiral Benbow. A place that most in this hamlet avoided since the arrival of that old sea-dog Billy Bones. Now it appeared there was more trouble –	*Notice the formality of the language to make it sound 'old English'.* *Use dashes to make a pause and add emphasis to the following words.*
only this time the name of Captain Flint was in the air. Just the name of Flint sent a shiver through any man's bones – mine included.	*Decide what the narrator might have done next. Remember the narrator can easily influence the emotions of the reader.*
I offered them a place to stay; I said I would accompany them in the other direction to Squire Trelawney's but not even three gold sovereigns would induce **him**	*Deliberate error to be picked up on the reread at the end – change from first to third person.*
to go to the inn. I could not persuade them to remain in the village and so **he** did the only thing **he** could. I gave young Jim my pistol to use to protect them both.	*Need to reread to make sure I have kept it in the first person.*

Resolution of a dilemma

Chapter 33, The Fall of a Chieftain

Well, there we stood, two on one side, five on the other, the pit between us, and nobody screwed up high enough to offer the first blow. Silver never moved; he watched them very upright on his crutch, and looked as cool as ever I saw him. He was brave, and no mistake. At last, Merry seemed to think a speech might help matters.

"Mates," says he, "there's two of them alone there; one's the old cripple that brought us all here and blundered us down to this; the other's that cub that I mean to have the heart of. Now, mates …"

He was raising his arm and his voice, and plainly meant to lead a charge. But just then, crack! crack! crack! three musket-shots flashed out of the thicket.

Merry tumbled head foremost into the excavation; the man with the bandage spun round like a teetotum, and fell all his length upon his side, where he lay dead, but still twitching; and the other three turned and ran for it with all their might.

Before you could wink, Long John had fired two barrels of a pistol into the struggling Merry; and as the man rolled up his eyes at him in the last agony, "George," said he, "I reckon I settled you." At the same moment the doctor, Gray, and Ben Gunn joined us, with smoking muskets, from among the nutmeg trees.

"Forward!" cried the doctor. "Double quick, my lads. We must head 'em off the boats."

(Exemplar analysis)

Example of analysis of *Resolution of a dilemma*

Dilemma reaches a pitch where it looks as though Jim and Silver are going to be killed.

The connective that leads into the resolution.

The following paragraphs go on to give details of the resolution. They were facing 5 pirates alone, now 1 is dead, 1 in treasure hole and 3 making run for boats.

Builds further tension, the fortunes of hero(es) are at the most critical point).

Typical resolution in a quest story: help arrives just in time.

Another pirate is killed by Silver.

They set off to deal with remaining three pirates.

Well, there we stood, two on one side, five on the other, the pit between us, and nobody screwed up high enough to offer the first blow. Silver never moved; he watched them very upright on his crutch, and looked as cool as ever I saw him. He was brave, and no mistake. At last, Merry seemed to think a speech might help matters.

"Mates," says he, "there's two of them alone there; one's the old cripple that brought us all here and blundered us down to this; the other's that cub that I mean to have the heart of. Now, mates ..."

He was raising his arm and his voice, and plainly meant to lead a charge. But just then, crack! crack! crack! three musket-shots flashed out of the thicket. Merry tumbled head foremost into the excavation; the man with the bandage spun round like a teetotum, and fell all his length upon his side, where he lay dead, but still twitching; and the other three turned and ran for it with all their might.

Before you could wink, Long John had fired two barrels of a pistol into the struggling Merry; and as the man rolled up his eyes at him in the last agony, "George," said he, "I reckon I settled you." At the same moment the doctor, Gray, and Ben Gunn joined us, with smoking muskets, from among the nutmeg trees.

"Forward!" cried the doctor. "Double quick, my lads. We must head 'em off the boats."

(Pupil copymaster)

Resolutions for you to analyse

Chapter 5, The Last of the Blind Man

Context: *The pirates have had the signal that danger approaches but they are arguing among themselves about searching the house for Jim and the Treasure Map.*

Squalling was the word for it, Pew's anger rose so high at these objections; till at last, his passion completely taking the upper hand, he struck at them right and left in his blindness, and his stick sounded heavily on more than one.

These, in their turn, cursed back at the blind miscreant, threatened him in horrid terms, and tried in vain to catch the stick and wrest it from his grasp.

This quarrel was the saving of us; for while it was still raging, another sound came from the top of the hill on the side of the hamlet, the tramp of horses galloping. Almost at the same time a pistol-shot, flash and report, came from the hedge-side. And that was plainly the last signal of danger; for the buccaneers turned at once and ran, separating in every direction, one seaward along the cove, one slant across the hill, and so on, so that in half a minute not a sign of them remained but Pew.

Chapter 24, The Cruise of the Coracle

Context: *Jim has cut the mooring ropes on the Hispaniola, fallen asleep in the coracle and woken to find a rough sea and no hope of getting back to land. He becomes increasingly thirsty and sees the ship. With great difficulty the coracle and the ship gradually come closer.*

And then, of a sudden, I began to comprehend. I had scarce time to think, scarce time to act and save myself. I was on the summit of one swell when the schooner came stooping over the next. The bowsprit was over my head. I sprang to my feet, and leaped, stamping the coracle under water. With one hand I caught the jib-boom, while my foot was lodged between the stay and the brace; and as I still clung there panting, a dull blow told me that the schooner had charged down upon and struck the coracle, and that I was left without retreat on the *Hispaniola*.

Chapter 28, In the Enemies' Camp

Context: *Jim has walked into the pirates at the stockade and is about to be killed by one of them.*

And he sprang up, drawing his knife as if he had been twenty.

"Avast, there!" cried Silver. "Who are you, Tom Morgan? Maybe you thought you was cap'n here, perhaps. By the powers, but I'll teach you better! Cross me, and you'll go where many a good man's gone before you, first and last, these thirty year back, some to the yard-arm, shiver my timbers! And some by the board, and all to feed the fishes. There's never a man looked me between the eyes and seen 'a good day afterwards, Tom Morgan, you may lay to that."

(Pupil copymaster)

A planning frame for writing resolutions

Dilemma	Resolution	Linking words and phrases to move from the dilemma to the resolution
Blind Pew and his pirates searching the Admiral Benbow for Bones' map. About to discover Jim and his mother hiding.		
Jim cuts the mooring rope to *Hispaniola* and falls asleep exhausted in Ben Gunn's boat. The sea becomes rough and Jim is in danger of drowning.		
Jim is captured by pirates and they want to kill him.		
The pirates find the treasure chest empty and turn on Long John Silver and Jim.		

(Pupil copymaster)

Stevenson's writing style

Squire Trelawney, Dr Livesey, and the rest of these gentlemen having asked me to write down the whole particulars about Treasure Island, from the beginning to the end, keeping nothing back but the bearings of the island, and that only because there is still treasure not yet lifted, I take up my pen in this year of grace 17– and go back to the time when my father kept the Admiral Benbow inn and the brown old seaman with the sabre cut first took up his lodging under our roof.

Context of the last paragraph: Trelawney and his crew stow the treasure safely in the Hispaniola's hold and leave provisions for the marooned pirates before setting sail for England. During a brief stop at a South American port, Silver, who faces trial and execution, steals a sack of coins and escapes over the rail.

Of Silver we have heard no more. That formidable seafaring man with one leg has at last gone clean out of my life; but I dare say he met his old Negress, and perhaps still lives in comfort with her and Capitan Flint. It is to be hoped so, I suppose, for his chances of comfort in another world are very small. The bar silver and the arms still lie, for all that I know, where Flint buried them; and certainly they shall lie there for me. Oxen and wain-ropes would not bring me back again to that accursed island; and the worst dreams that I ever have are when I hear the surf booming about its coasts or start upright in bed with the sharp voice of Captain Flint still ringing in my ears, "Pieces of eight! Pieces of eight!"

(Exemplar analysis)

Example of analysis of Stevenson's style

Old-fashioned language and expressions (examples underlined).

Present perfect participle.

Squire Trelawney, Dr Livesey, and the rest of these gentlemen having asked me to write down the whole particulars about Treasure Island, from the beginning to the end, keeping nothing back but the bearings of the island, and that only because there is still treasure not yet lifted, I take up my pen in this year of grace 17– and go back to the time when my father kept the Admiral Benbow inn and the brown old seaman with the sabre cut first took up his lodging under our roof.

Note length of the sentences:
● count the clauses
● note the number of commas
● discuss where you could have split the sentence into two or three shorter ones.

Note sentence structure.

Use of semi-colons to separate parts of a sentence. It marks a greater pause than a comma.

Old-fashioned language and expressions (examples underlined).

Of Silver we have heard no more. That formidable seafaring man with one leg has at last gone clean out of my life; but I dare say he met his old Negress, and perhaps still lives in comfort with her and Capitan Flint. It is to be hoped so, I suppose, for his chances of comfort in another world are very small. The bar silver and the arms still lie, for all that I know, where Flint buried them; and certainly they shall lie there for me. Oxen and wain-ropes would not bring me back again to that accursed island; and the worst dreams that I ever have are when I hear the surf booming about its coasts or start upright in bed with the sharp voice of Captain Flint still ringing in my ears, "Pieces of eight! Pieces of eight!"

Many pirates at this time were based in the West Indies and married local women. It was not a pejorative term.

Different spelling.

Long sentences (many commas and semi-colons to end clauses).

(Exemplar material)

Example of modelling an alternative ending in Stevenson's style

Write this on the board ...	... while you are saying this
Once on board, the formidable sea-faring	*Use old-fashioned words taken from other parts of the story.*
man with one leg again took me into his confidence;	*Use semi-colon to separate clauses and give a longer pause.*
without realising, I soon fell again under his enticing spell.	*Long sentence with many clauses using commas.*
He told me of his thoughts to leave the ship when it came alongside	*Nautical term to remind readers that LJS was a seaman.*
in a port in South America	*Reference taken from the actual text.*
and join his Negress.	*Reference taken from the actual text.*
An invitation to come along was proffered to me	*Passive tense makes it seem more formal. Use of old-fashioned word.*
to run my own Admiral Benbow; provided for, of course, by the proceeds of Captain Flint's treasure hoard.	

(Exemplar analysis)

Example of analysis of a film review of *Shrek*

Opinions of the reviewer.

Indicates the genre of the film.

Who it appeals to and why.

Technical information about the film given here, for example, feats of bravery by camera operator to get the shots, the close ups, the way the director chose to film certain scenes, the costumes, the musical score.

Give own opinion.

Stunning animation and rib-splitting humour are two of the characteristics of this recently released film.

This is a traditional children's fairy tale with a twist. It will appeal to children of all ages. The youngest will enjoy the wonderful animated characters, while older children and adults will understand the jokes and animation on a different level.

In order to become king, Lord Farquaad needs to marry a princess. Shrek, a feared ogre, is persuaded to rescue Princess Fiona from a castle protected by molten lava and a dragon. Shrek is helped, or more accurately hindered, by his new annoying sidekick, a talking donkey.

The animation is very realistic. The music chosen for the soundtrack just adds to the overall impact of the film, which is a real entertaining feast full of visual hi-jinks and energy. None of the characters weaken the plot.

I would recommend this film to everyone who enjoys a good laugh!

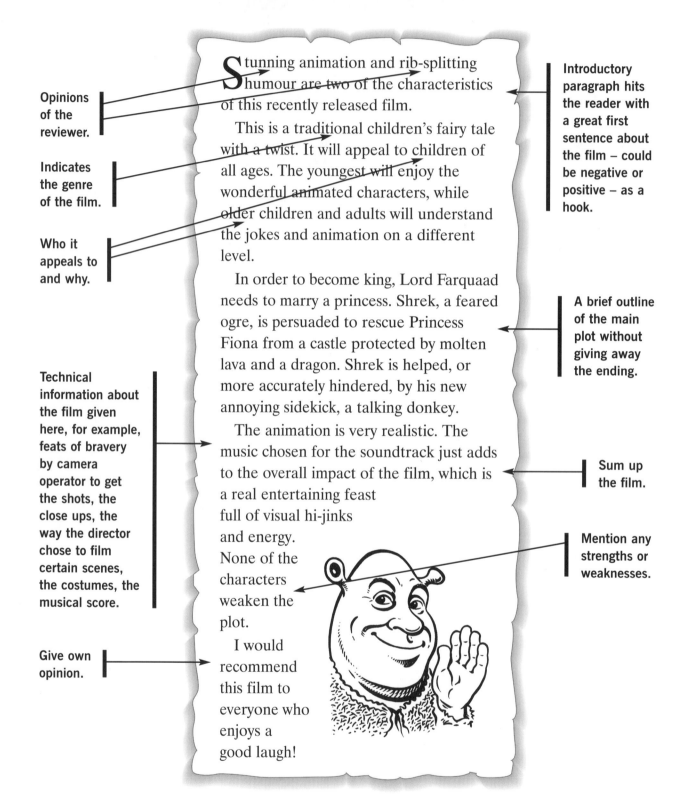

Introductory paragraph hits the reader with a great first sentence about the film – could be negative or positive – as a hook.

A brief outline of the main plot without giving away the ending.

Sum up the film.

Mention any strengths or weaknesses.

Classworks Literacy Year 6 © Paula Ross, Nelson Thornes Ltd 2003

(Exemplar material)

Planning frame for a film review of *Treasure Island*

Hook the reader	Pirates, treasure, swashbuckling, thrilling
Genre	Adventure
Audience	Children/whole family
Summary without the ending	— Jim Hawkins gets hold of treasure map — Delivers map to Squire Trelawney — Sets off for Treasure Island — Crew are pirates led by Long John Silver — Mutiny plan to take the treasure themselves — Jim intervenes: a series of adventures on Treasure Island with marooned Ben Gunn — Ever closer to the treasure
Technical details	— Live action adaptation of classic book — Produced in a studio not on location, not very realistic sets — Music/sound effects — build tension
Opinions/comments	— Weaknesses: no women in the film; dated; ending changed from the book (weaknesses) — Strengths: entertaining; helps to clarify the 'old' language in the book

A synopsis of the book's climax for reworking as playscript

The men start off again, and as they near the tree under which the treasure has been buried, they become very excited but when they finally get near the spot of the buried treasure, they suddenly stop. In front of them is a very large hole, dug some time ago, which contains the shaft of a broken pick and parts of packing-cases, on which the name of Flint's ship, Walrus, is branded. The treasure has gone!

Naturally, the pirates are stunned by the lack of the fortune. The first to recover is Long John Silver, who hands Jim a pistol and moves so that the hole is between the five seaman and Jim and himself. Silver now behaves in a friendly manner toward Jim, a stark change from his early antagonistic behaviour. The seamen jump into the pit and dig with their fingers, searching frantically for any gold at all. In a frenzy, George Merry screams at Silver and accuses him of knowing all along that the treasure had gone from the spot on the map.

Bravely, Silver faces the five remaining men and as Merry prepares to lead a charge against him, there are three musket-shots from the thicket. Merry tumbles, wounded, into the pit, another man falls down dead, and the three left turn and run. Silver shoots and kills Merry, just as the doctor, Gray, and Ben Gunn appear. The doctor urges everyone to chase the seamen and head them off from the boats.

(Exemplar material)

Example of rethinking narrative for playscript

Write this on the board ...	... while you are saying this
In the rain forest	*Decide the stage instructions.*
Long John Silver, Jim Hawkins, the 5 pirates including George Merry	*Decide the characters.*
Where the men are standing and what are they doing: one or two could have hands to eye looking for the tree; two looking at the map together and pointing; Long John Silver looking round furtively; Jim is keeping quiet trying not to be noticed by the other pirates.	*Decide the stage directions.*
The men start off again,	*Need someone to speak to get the action moving again, tone of voice important – building excitement and becoming more impatient.*
and as they near the tree under which the treasure has been buried, they become very excited	*Speeding up, talking loudly among themselves, words of encouragement, pushing Long John Silver out of the way.*
but when they finally get near the spot of the buried treasure, they suddenly stop.	*Shock and horror on their faces, speech is now very much slower and broken.*
In front of them is a very large hole, dug some time ago,	*Speech needed to tell the audience they can see the empty hole.*
which contains the shaft of a broken pick and parts of packing-cases, on which the name of Flint's ship, *Walrus*, is branded.	*Scenery required.*
The treasure has gone!	

(Exemplar material)

Example of modelling narrative into playscript

Original narrative text	Transformed into playscript	Commentary
	SCENE: A very hot, steamy rainforest.	*Use of colon to separate subtitle from the text*
	Stage left, 5 pirates are very animated as they consult the treasure map; two are looking out towards the distance, hands cupped across their foreheads.	*Stage instructions – setting.*
	Long John Silver with his back to the rest looks distractedly towards the shore while Jim cowers down half out of sight a little way from Long John Silver.	*Stage directions for actions.*
	Stage right, parts of packing-cases, with the name Walrus.	*Instructions written in present tense.*
The men start off again,	Merry: (authoritatively) **Right, me hearties, 'tis this way, follow me.** (Beckons and sets off.)	
	(A few moments later as they approach tree)	*Leave space between each character's speech.*
and as they near the tree under which the treasure has been buried, they become very excited	Morgan: (shouting and running excitedly) **Yes, yes, there it is. Flint's treasure – it's ours.**	
	Dick: **I can feel the gold pouring through my fingers already.** (Pushes Silver out of the way and runs after Morgan.)	
	Silver: (Jims helps him to his feet) **So that's it, is it? Now you see the treasure, I can be pushed aside. We'll see …**	
	Captain Flint: (perched on Silver's shoulder) **Pieces of eight, pieces of eight!**	

but when they finally get near the spot of the buried treasure, they suddenly stop.
  In front of them is a very large hole, dug some time ago, which contains the shaft of a broken pick and parts of packing-cases, on which the name of Flint's ship, *Walrus*, is branded.
  The treasure has gone!
	(The 5 pirates pull up sharp, almost falling over each other.)	

	Merry: (unbelievingly) **The treasure …**	
	Morgan: (desperate) **Where is it?**	
	Dick: **It's gone!**	

Exemplar material

Checklists for classic fiction

Example of a checklist for summary of a book   ①

- Mention the author's name in the first sentence

- Use chronological order

- Use the present tense

- Use many time and sequencing connectives

- Ensure that it is a factual account

- Do not include your own opinions or feelings about the book

- Reduce the details of the chapters to just one or two main points

- Link some chapters together and take one or two points from all of them

- Take care not to change the order or balance of the original work

Example of a checklist for analysing dialogue ②

- There should be a new paragraph for each new speaker

- Speech marks show the words spoken

- Punctuation needed before the closing speech marks

- Interjections – for example, 'well then', 'now' – are used to make speech more realistic

- Contracted forms of verbs used, for example, 'we'd', 'I'll'

- Colloquialisms used, for example, 'matey', 'me hearties'

Example of a checklist for writing your own dialogue ③

- Hear the character speaking the dialogue in your head

- Make sure that each character has his/her/its own voice

- Don't overuse speech verbs, for example, 'muttered'

- Don't overuse speech adverbs, for example, 'excitedly', 'nervously'

- Don't keep referring to the characters by their names but make sure the reader knows who is speaking

- Use dashes to show a pause or an aside

Continued ...

(Exemplar material)

More checklists and a model for classic fiction

Example of modelled dialogue

He threw his crutch so hard against the tree that the birds took to flight in fear.

"What's the matter?" Gunn asked knowingly.

"What have you done with the treasure, you – numbskull?"

- Reader knows who the unnamed speaker is (Silver) through the clue of his crutch

- Mood is set through the action and dialogue working together

- Tone is set through the author's choice of language, e.g. 'knowingly', 'numbskull'

- Reader is given a deeper understanding of the plot and characters

- Speech sounds realistic

- Dialogue shows what is happening

- Dialogue is used instead of writing a lengthy paragraph to describe the scene

- Contraction: 'What's the matter?' – speech is faster than written word and contractions help author convey this

- Dashes show a pause in the speech

Example of a checklist for writing in Stevenson's style

- Use old-fashioned language

- Include sentences with several clauses

- Separate clauses with commas and semi-colons

- Use passive tense for formality

- Vary the language depending on whether it is a pirate or a gentleman speaking

Example of a checklist for a film review

- Hook the reader with a strong first sentence about the film

- Include the genre

- State who it appeals to (the audience)

- Give a summary without the ending

- Give technical details

- Give opinion of the reviewer

- Mention strengths and weaknesses, for example, the plot, acting, costumes

Example of a checklist of playscript features ⑦

- Stage instructions describe the setting

- Dialogue is set out exactly as the characters speak it (direct speech)

- No speech marks are needed

- Stage directions (written in brackets) tell the actor how to speak the lines

- Stage directions (written in brackets) give instructions for the action

- Character names are set out in the margin, followed by a colon – for example, Jim:

- Technical vocabulary is used, for example, 'Move stage left'

- Stage direction and instructions are given in the present tense

- There should be spacing between different characters' lines

(Marking ladder)

Marking ladder for a chapter summary

Name: _____

Pupil	Objective	Teacher
	I noted the title and number of chapter.	
	My text is in chronological order.	
	It is written in the present tense.	
	I used at least three time and sequencing connectives: 1) 2) 3)	
	It is a factual account.	
	I reduced the details of the chapter to just the main points.	
	I used very little descriptive language.	
	I included at least three complex sentences.	
	My summary does not change the order or balance of the original work.	
	What could I do to improve my writing next time?	

(Marking ladder)

Marking ladder for writing dialogue

Name: _____

Pupil	Objective	Teacher
	My dialogue between the characters moves the story on: • it develops the characters • it shows the reader what is happening.	
	My dialogue sounds realistic – the characters have their own voices.	
	I used contractions, for example, 'I'd'.	
	I used interjections, for example, 'Well, um'.	
	I used dashed to show pauses.	
	I used colloquialisms.	
	My punctuation is accurate: • I used a new paragraph for a new speaker • I used speech marks around the spoken words • I used punctuation before the final speech mark each time • I omitted speech marks at a full stop if the same person continued to talk.	
	What could I do to improve my dialogue writing next time?	

(Marking ladder)

Marking ladder for modern version of a quest story

Name: _____

Pupil	Objective	Teacher
	I established the task – to find something.	
	I revealed the setting.	
	My characters set off and overcome obstacles en route.	
	The dilemma(s) is (are): • Can't find it • Can't get in • Get trapped • Get chased.	
	The solutions to the dilemmas are realistic.	
	My characters arrive back at the start, task accomplished.	
	I included an ending, for example, a final comment.	
	I used dialogue for characterisation or showing the reader what is happening.	
	I used two narrators.	
	What could I do to improve my planning of a quest story next time?	

(Marking ladder)

Marking ladder for a film review

Name: _____

Pupil	Objective	Teacher
	My review hooks the reader with a strong first sentence about the film.	
	I included the genre.	
	I stated who it appeals to (the audience).	
	I gave a summary of the action without the ending.	
	I gave technical details.	
	I gave my own opinion as the reviewer.	
	I mentioned strengths and weaknesses, for example, the plot, acting, costumes.	
	What could I do to improve my review next time?	

(Marking ladder)

Marking ladder for transforming narrative into playscript

Name: _____

Pupil	Objective	Teacher
	I changed description into stage instructions to describe the setting.	
	I added dialogue to tell the audience what is happening.	
	I left out some parts of the narrative (give example).	
	I set out the dialogue as direct speech.	
	My stage directions are written in brackets: • to tell the actors how to speak their lines • to give instructions for the action.	
	My stage directions are in present tense.	
	What could I do to improve my playscript next time?	

Non-chronological Reports

Outcome

Information leaflets on mountain ranges, including comparative reports (cross-curricular link to QCA topic 'Mountains')

Objectives

Sentence

1 to revise from Y5 the conventions of standard English.

4 to investigate connecting words and phrases.

5 to form complex sentences.

Text

12 to comment critically on the language, style, success of examples of non-fiction such as periodicals, reviews, reports, leaflets.

13 to secure understanding of the features of non-chronological reports: introductions to orientate reader; use of generalisations to categorise; language to describe and differentiate; impersonal language; mostly present tense.

17 to write non-chronological reports linked to other subjects.

18 to use IT to plan, revise, edit writing to improve accuracy and conciseness and bring it to publication standard e.g. through compiling a class newspaper, and presentation.

Planning frame

- Define non-chronological report and identify the key features.
- Explore methods used to plan a comparative report.
- Change planning into written outcome: first paragraph to orientate reader; central paragraphs of information; summarising conclusion
- Use ICT to present the report as a leaflet using DTP software.

How you could plan this unit

Day 1	Day 2	Day 3	Day 4	Day 5
Reading and analysis	**Reading, modelling and writing**	**Reading and analysis** Read, analyse and annotate first paragraphs	**Modelling and writing** Using ICT: write first paragraph to orientate the reader. Include generalisations	**Reading and analysis** Read, analyse and annotate main paragraphs. Analyse the role of illustrations, diagrams, maps and so on
Some Examples	*Preparing Information*			

Day 6	Day 7	Day 8	Day 9	Day 10
Modelling and writing Central paragraphs	**Reading and analysis**	**Modelling and writing**	**Reading, analysis, modelling and writing** Analyse and annotate final paragraphs. Model and write a concluding summary	**Writing and editing** Use marking ladder
	Planning a Report	*Report Writing*		

Some Examples

Objective

We will explore the purpose of a non-chronological text, and learn how to identify texts that are non-chronological and their features

You need: Resource Pages A–C, and K; fiction and non-fiction books, including encyclopaedias, leaflets, brochures, magazines; strips of paper for display; highlighters, coloured pencils; Blu-tack™.

Whole class work

- Begin with the starter 'Mind map' on page 197.

- Tell the children the focus for this work is non-chronological reports. The outcome for the work will be leaflets about three different mountain ranges. *Using the knowledge you have about the prefix 'chrono', what do you think a non-chronological report is?*

- Explain that these are reports that do not refer to a time sequence, but where the information is organised by linking together similar attributes and characteristics. Example texts include: non-fiction books, tourist guidebooks, information leaflets.

- Display some of the pages from these types of book and revise the layout and features:

> title page
> contents
> index
> information to be dipped into rather than read cover to cover
> use of photos, diagrams, illustrations

- Distribute the selection of books. Ask the children to decide which show non-chronological writing. *How do you know?*

- Read Resource Page A. *What did you notice about how the paragraphs are organised?* Answer: each one is about a different aspect of the Andes Mountains.

- Analyse and annotate the text (see Resource Page B).
  - the first paragraph indicates what the report is about and classifies the information
  - clear and logically ordered paragraphs of linked information
  - facts not opinions
  - uses a formal style (no personal pronouns)
  - uses present tense
  - uses precise descriptive and technical language.

- As the features are noted, ask the children to write them on sentence strips and display as a class checklist (see Resource Page K for ideas).

Independent, pair or guided work

- Read Resource Page C. Decide whether this is a non-chronological report and, if so, why.

- The children analyse and annotate features using highlighters/pencils or underlining.

Plenary

- Display Resource Page A. Ask the children to Blu-tack™ the features on sentence strips on to the text. Ensure that they are able to explain each of the features as they annotate the text.

Preparing Information

Objectives

We will skim and scan text for relevant information. We will collect, organise and classify information, and then prepare a plan for non-chronological writing

You need: Resource Pages A, D, K; Post-it™ notes; a selection of books and other materials about mountains.

Whole class work

- Explain that today they are going to learn how to plan a non-chronological report.

- Display Resource Page A. *What is the main focus of this report?* Write the answer in the centre circle of the spidergram (Resource Page D). Continue modelling the spidergram, adding the topic for each paragraph to a Post-it™ note before sticking it on one of the surrounding circles.

- Tell the children that after choosing paragraphs, the writer needs to order the information. Demonstrate ordering the Post-it™ notes on the board; change your mind and reorder. *Will the writer need to do anything before planning the report?* (Answer: research the topic.)

- Teaching the children how to plan before researching the topic will help them to select information more effectively.

- Select a mountain range. Revise how to collect information using book titles, contents and indices, subtitles, CD-ROMs, leaflets and appropriate Internet sites.

- Decide on the likely sections for the report: climate, wildlife, vegetation, activities. Write each one on a Post-it™ note. Remember to include an initial paragraph that gives general information.

- Remind the children how to skim and scan the text (see Autobiography and Diaries, page 23). Model adding a few notes from the text to the appropriate Post-it™ note.

- Put the paragraphs into the most effective order. Decide if any of the sections needs a subsection.

Independent, pair or guided work

- Working in small groups, the children choose three mountain ranges to research. Each child or pair of children researches one of the three mountain ranges and decides on the paragraphs for the report.

- The children write a title for each paragraph on a Post-it™ note and arrange as a spidergram.

- Add research notes to each paragraph Post-it™.

Plenary

- Show the spidergrams to the other members of the group. Decide together:
  - *Are the paragraphs appropriate for an information leaflet about the selected mountain range?*
  - *Have the other members of the group come up with similar paragraphs?*
  - *Should any paragraph titles be changed?*
  - *Is the relevant information in the correct paragraph?*
  - *Do any of the sections need sub-paragraphs?*

106

Planning a Report

Objective

We will skim and scan text for relevant information, and then prepare a planning grid for a comparative report

You need: Resource Pages E–I.

Whole class work

- *In this lesson you will learn how to select facts so you can write a report comparing the impact of tourists on the environment in the Lake District and the Himalayas.*

- Review the planning from the previous lesson. Point out the section about the effects of tourists. Explain that the children are going to compare the negative effects of tourism on different mountain ranges in order to conclude whether problems are distinct to a particular area or are likely to affect all mountainous regions.

- Share the two texts (Resource Pages E and G). Tell the children that in order to make a comparison, you need to group similar facts together. Model highlighting the facts about the number of people visiting the two areas (see Resource Pages F and H).

- *What other similarities can you see between the areas?* Highlight in different colours as the children identify the points.

- Explain that a planning frame is a useful way of comparing two or more items. Using Resource Page I, model how to set up the frame with two columns for the Lake District and the Himalayas. Enter suitable headings for each area of information: travel, litter and so on. Add appropriate notes for the Lake District column.

- Ask the children to see if there are other problems seen in one area but not the other (for example, deforestation of the lower slopes of the Himalayas). Add a title to the planning frame: Exploitation of resources.

Independent, pair or guided work

- Ask the children to complete the planning frame for the Himalayas.
- Use other materials available in the classroom or on the Internet for information about a third mountain range.

Plenary

- *How can a planning frame help you to write a comparative report?* Answers could include:

> Writing an introductory sentence: the report is about man causing many problems to the mountain environment.
>
> Organising paragraphs logically in the report: the problems become the paragraphs.
>
> Writing a conclusion to the report: two completely different mountain ranges suffer similar problems caused by man.

Report Writing

Objectives

We will write a sub-section of the leaflet as a comparative report. We will then use notes from a planning frame to write a comparative report

You need: Resource Pages I–K; class display list of connectives.

Whole class work

- *In this lesson you will turn your planning frame points into a report section*.

- Display the completed planning frame (Resource Page I) and review the sections.

- Using checklist 1 (Resource Page K), remind the children that the report will need to include these.

- Model writing the comparative report (Resource Page J). Emphasise the use of words/phrases to link statements:

  > connectives for comparison – 'also', 'in the same way', 'likewise', 'similarly'
  >
  > connectives for contrast – 'although', 'and yet', 'in contrast'
  >
  > connectives for addition – 'also', 'equally important', 'furthermore', 'in addition'

- Remind the children that this is just one section of their report and as such will be quite short. If computers are available, the comparative report could be modelled directly on screen. Remind the children of the previous lesson's plenary where they gave their ideas on how the planning frame would help to write the report:
  - writing an introductory sentence: the report is about man causing many problems to the mountain environment
  - organising paragraphs logically in the report: the problems become the paragraphs
  - writing a conclusion to the report: two completely different mountain ranges suffer similar problems caused by man.

- Review the use of connectives in the modelled text and add them to the class list.

Independent, pair or guided work

- The children choose one activity from the following (more able children may complete several):
  - Write their own report from planning frames.
  - Write the paragraph about the impact man has on the mountain areas.
  - Add details about a third mountain range into the modelled writing.

Plenary

- Refer to checklist 1 (Resource Page K). Ask the children to highlight/underline/use colour to pick out features in their own work as you call them out from the checklist.

- Ask one or two children to read their work aloud. The rest of the class identify features of report writing in the work.

Exemplar material

The Andes

ANDES, the principal mountains of South America and one of the greatest mountain systems of the world. The Andes include some of the world's highest peaks. More than 50 of them soar higher than 6 100 m (20 000 ft) above sea level. Only the Himalayas of south central Asia are higher. The mountains reach into seven countries: Venezuela, Colombia, Ecuador, Peru, Bolivia, Chile, and Argentina.

The climate in the Andes varies greatly. In general, the northern section is rainy and warm; the central section is dry, with great extremes of temperature; and the southern section is rainy and cool.

In the northern Andes and in parts of the central Andes, evergreen tropical rain forest covers the lower slopes. In the southern Andes, broadleaf and coniferous trees cover the lower slopes. Above the timberline are treeless highland meadows, but the high plateaus of the central Andes support only a sparse covering of grasses and stunted shrubs.

The most important native domestic animal of the Andes is the llama, a member of the same family as the camel. The llama, found predominantly in Peru and Bolivia, can live at high altitudes. It is used as a beast of burden and yields wool, milk, and meat. The alpaca, an animal related to the llama, is raised for its wool. The birds of the Andes include the condor, the largest of all birds of prey.

The people of the Andes have adapted their lifestyles to cope with the range of terrain, climate, vegetation and wildlife that the mountain range offers.

from Encarta *(abridged and edited)*

(Exemplar analysis)

Example of analysis of *The Andes*

General comment to start, classifying the mountains as one of the greatest mountain systems of the world. (<u>Facts are underlined.</u>)

Goes on to explain why they are one of the greatest mountain systems.

Uses precise descriptive language (examples in italics).

The report is ordered logically so it is easy to follow: classifying information, climate, vegetation, animal life.

ANDES, <u>the principal mountains of South America</u> and one of the greatest mountain systems of the world. The Andes <u>include some of the world's highest peaks. More than 50 of them soar higher than 6 100 m (20 000 ft) above sea level. Only the Himalayas of south central Asia are higher. The mountains reach into seven countries: Venezuela, Colombia, Ecuador, Peru, Bolivia, Chile, and Argentina</u>.

The climate in the Andes varies greatly. In general, the northern section is rainy and warm; the central section is dry, with great extremes of temperature; and the southern section is rainy and cool.

In the northern Andes and in parts of the central Andes, evergreen tropical rain forest covers the lower slopes. In the southern Andes, broadleaf and coniferous trees cover the lower slopes. Above the timberline are *treeless highland meadows*, but the high plateaus of the central Andes support only *a sparse covering of grasses and stunted shrubs*.

The most important *native domestic animal* of the Andes is the llama, a member of the same family as the <u>camel</u>. The llama, found predominantly in Peru and Bolivia, can live at high altitudes. It is used as a beast of burden and yields wool, milk, and meat. The alpaca, an animal related to the llama, is raised for its wool. The birds of the Andes include the <u>condor</u>, the largest of all birds of prey.

The people of the Andes have adapted their lifestyles to cope with the range of terrain, climate, vegetation and wildlife that the mountain range offers.

from Encarta *(abridged and edited)*

Opening paragraph gives a clear indication of what the report will be about.

Use of technical language.

Use of present tense.

Report is formal, no personal pronouns used.

Some paragraphs have implicit sub-titles: this one is 'Climate'.

A concluding sentence that summarises the information in the report.

(Pupil copymaster)

The Himalayas web page (abridged)

Destination: NEPAL

Nepal is a landlocked country with a total land area of 147 181 sq km (56 136 sq miles). The country is bordered by the People's Republic of China to the north and the Republic of India to the south, east and west. The world's highest peak Mt Sagarmatha (Everest), 8 848 m (29 028 ft) lies in Nepal. Its capital is Kathmandu.

Nepal's climate ranges from tropical to Arctic depending upon the altitude. The Terai region has a hot humid climate. The midland regions are pleasant almost all the year round, although winter nights are cool. The northern mountain region, at an altitude above 3 353m has an alpine climate with a considerably lower temperature in winter. The main rainy season is during the monsoon period (June to September) with rainfall of over 56 inches a year.

The geography of Nepal is blessed with a number of small and large rivers. Three main river systems – Kosi, Gandaki and Karnali – originate in the Himalayas, flow southward and empty into the Ganges. Nepal has been a habitat of different rare species of flora and fauna. In order to protect the fragile eco-system, Nepal has set up thirteen national parks and wildlife reserves in different parts of the country.

Nepal has a population of more than 18 million, made up of different races and tribes, living in different regions, wearing different costumes and speaking different languages and dialects. The Sherpas live in the Himalayan region up to an altitude of 4 570m. Hinduism and Buddhism constitute the two major religions of Nepal. As Nepal is the birthplace of Lord Buddha, it is one of the major attractions for Buddhists all over the world. The mountains of Nepal play a vital role in the lifestyle of the Nepali people.

http://www.hotels-world.com/travelinfo/as/nepal/country.htm

(Exemplar material)

Spidergram for modelled planning

Stage 1: When the children answer **What was the main focus of the text?** Write, 'The Andes mountain range' in the centre of a circle drawn in the centre of the board.

Stage 2: Surround the central circle with linked circles. Place a Post-it™ in each circle, labelled with the focus of each paragraph.

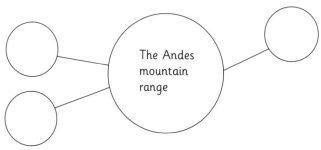

Stage 3: Explain that some paragraphs may have a lot of information and they could be split again – add smaller circles as below.

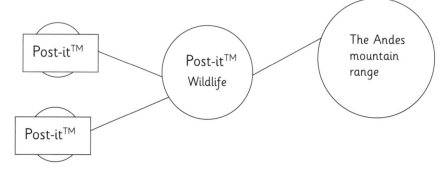

Stage 4: Decide the order you will write the paragraphs in and number the outside circles accordingly. Post-its™ allow changes of mind and easy reordering of paragraphs.

A spidergram may look like this.

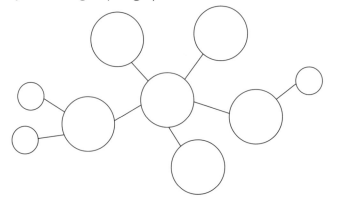

Classworks Literacy Year 6 © Paula Ross, Nelson Thornes Ltd 2003

The Lake District

The Lake District is a particularly popular national park that is visited by more and more people each year. This is due to the improvements in roads, such as fast motorways in the area and the increasing number of car owners. They come to see and experience the fantastic scenery. This is placing an ever-greater pressure on the mountain environment.

The difficulty is for the authorities to help preserve the beauty of the mountains without lowering the enjoyment of the visitors.

Traffic jams on the roads leading to and within the Lake District both disturb the peace and create air pollution. Parking facilities at the most popular sites, such as Balanced Rock and the Windows, are filled to capacity in peak season, causing visitors to park on the grass verges which in turn causes soil erosion. Litter is also a problem, although there are many bins and people are encouraged to take their litter home.

Activities such as hiking, camping, climbing and especially in recent years, mountain biking, cause much footpath erosion, wearing away paths, endangering and destroying the vegetation. Nesting birds and animals may be disturbed and water courses can become polluted. Visitors often leave the established trails, trampling on delicate areas that are home to a whole host of micro-organisms and will take years to recover.

In addition to this, the traditional hill farming of the Lake District has effects on the landscape. The sheep put out to graze on the upper fells keep the grass short and eat the other vegetation, which includes young saplings.

Classworks Literacy Year 6 © Paula Ross, Nelson Thornes Ltd 2003

(Exemplar analysis)

Example of analysis of *The Lake District*

Numbers of people – see bold text.

Travel to and around the area – see italic text.

Effect on the eco-system – see bold italic text.

The Lake District is a particularly popular national park that **is visited by more and more people each year**. This is due to the *improvements in roads, such as fast motorways in the area and the increasing number of car owners*. They come to see and experience the fantastic scenery. This is placing an ever-greater pressure on the mountain environment.

The difficulty is for the authorities to help preserve the beauty of the mountains without lowering the enjoyment of the visitors.

Traffic jams on the roads leading to and within the Lake District both disturb the peace and create air pollution. *Parking facilities at the most popular sites*, such as Balanced Rock and the Windows, *are filled to capacity* in peak season, causing *visitors to park on the grass verges* which in turn causes soil erosion. Litter is also a problem, although there are many bins and people are encouraged to take their litter home.

Activities such as **hiking, camping, climbing** and especially in recent years, **mountain biking**, cause **much footpath erosion, wearing away paths, endangering and destroying the vegetation. Nesting birds and animals may be disturbed and water courses can become polluted**. Visitors often leave the established trails, **trampling on delicate areas** that are home to a whole host of micro-organisms and will take years to recover.

In addition to this, the traditional hill farming of the Lake District has effects on the landscape. The sheep put out to graze on the upper fells keep the grass short and eat the other vegetation, which includes young saplings.

Litter – see text underlined in grey.

Traditional way of life – see underlined text.

(Pupil copymaster)

The Himalayas

Man has also been responsible to a large extent for some of the environmental problems faced by the mountains. Over the centuries, pilgrims and explorers have visited the mountains. However, in the past their numbers were few and the Himalayas were able to cope with the effects of human exploration in the areas.

But today, the story is different. In the last few decades, an intricate network of roads has been built into the mountains, which have made some of the most remote areas more easily accessible. This has translated into a tremendous increase in the numbers of people who visit the mountains every year. In 1994, more than 325 000 tourists visited Nepal, compared with around 46 000 in 1970.

The trekkers and climbers are causing many problems. Above 4 000 metres, vegetation grows at a snail's pace. Continual walking over the vegetation is causing soil erosion as the vegetation has no time to recover between tourist visits. Moreover, the average trekking group consumes 10 times more firewood per day than a local Sherpa family.

The Himalayas are now being exploited to provide materials for the growing number of forest-based industries.

For centuries, the hillside village of Namche Bazar – the gateway to the Mount Everest region – has been renowned as a market centre. Even today, a few traders still travel across the snowpeaks from as far away as Tibet and surrounding hills to barter salt and yak meat for rice, millet and other goods from the south. But lodge owners from across the region also travel to the Saturday market to pick up supplies for the tourist trade: peanut butter, Mars and Snickers bars, and rolls and rolls of toilet paper.

Although mountaineering expeditions have come regularly to Mount Everest and other peaks since Edmund Hillary and Tenzing Norgay's ascent in 1953, it was only five years ago that the first Nepali organised clean-up of the base camp site brought out 500 yak loads – 30 000 kilograms worth – of leftover rubbish.

People who used to work in the fields, who used to tend yaks are now working as guides and assisting tourists so there is also an indirect impact on the traditional lifestyle of the Sherpa people.

(Exemplar analysis)

Example of analysis of *The Himalayas*

Travel to and around the area – see italic text.

Numbers of people – see bold text.

Man has also been responsible to a large extent for some of the environmental problems faced by the mountains. Over the centuries, pilgrims and explorers have visited the mountains. However, in the past **their numbers were few** and the Himalayas were able to cope with the effects of human exploration in the areas.

But *today, the story is different. In the last few decades, an intricate network of roads has been built into the mountains, which have made some of the most remote areas more easily accessible.* This has translated into **a tremendous increase in the numbers of people who visit** the mountains every year. **In 1994, more than 325 000 tourists visited Nepal, compared with around 46 000 in 1970.**

The trekkers and climbers are causing many problems. ***Above 4 000 metres, vegetation grows at a snail's pace. Continual walking over the vegetation is causing soil erosion as the vegetation has no time to recover between tourist visits.*** Moreover, the average trekking group consumes 10 times more firewood per day than a local Sherpa family.

The Himalayas are now being exploited to provide materials for the growing number of forest-based industries.

Effect on eco-system – see bold italic text.

Exploitation of the area's resources by industry and visitors.

Point out this section last as there is not a similar section in the Lake District text.

For centuries, the hillside village of Namche Bazar – the gateway to the Mount Everest region – has been renowned as a market centre. Even today, a few traders still travel across the snowpeaks from as far away as Tibet and surrounding hills to barter salt and yak meat for rice, millet and other goods from the south. But lodge owners from across the region also travel to the Saturday market to pick up supplies for the tourist trade: peanut butter, Mars and Snickers bars, and rolls and rolls of toilet paper.

Litter – see text underlined in grey.

Although mountaineering expeditions have come regularly to Mount Everest and other peaks since Edmund Hillary and Tenzing Norgay's ascent in 1953, it was only five years ago that the first Nepali organised clean-up of the base camp site brought out 500 yak loads – 30 000 kilograms worth – of leftover rubbish.

Traditional way of life – see underlined text.

People who used to work in the fields, who used to tend yaks are now working as guides and assisting tourists so there is also an indirect impact on the traditional lifestyle of the Sherpa people.

(Exemplar material)

Example of a modelled planning frame

	Lake District	**The Himalayas** *(the children complete this during independent work)*
Visitors	• More and more people each year	• *Used to be occasional pilgrims and explorers* • *Increasing numbers visiting as travel gets easier*
Travel to/in mountains	• Better roads • More people own cars	• *New roads built to remote places*
Vegetation	• Destroyed by cars parking on verges • Destroyed by hikers leaving trails	• *Constant trekking* • *Vegetation grows very slowly*
Litter	• Some rubbish • Bins etc provided	• *Major problem – produced by climbers* • *Also tourists expecting to buy Western products etc*
Traditional life	• Hill farming – sheep eat important vegetation as well as the grass	• *Sherpa people's life is changing*
Exploitation of natural resources *(add this heading after completing the details for the Lake District)*		• *Using the forest from the lower slopes will cause problems: erosion* • *Using 10 x more wood than local families*

Classworks Literacy Year 6 © Paula Ross, Nelson Thornes Ltd 2003

(Exemplar material)

Example of modelling report writing

Decide how the report will be organised:

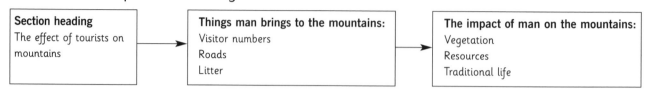

Section heading	**Things man brings to the mountains:**	**The impact of man on the mountains:**
The effect of tourists on mountains	Visitor numbers Roads Litter	Vegetation Resources Traditional life

Write this on the board ...	... while you are saying this
	Opening sentence needs to orientate the reader. Also needs to hook the reader and show the seriousness of the problem
One of the greatest dangers to the mountain ranges of the world is	*Present tense*
Man. It can be seen	*Use formal language*
that people affect the mountain regions of the Lake District and the Himalayas in two main ways, by what is	*Do not use personal pronouns*
brought to the area and what is done to the area when people are there.	*Need to continue by combining several pieces of information from the grid. Review the notes and decide to link visitors with roads and write a separate sentence about rubbish*
<u>Both</u> the Lake District <u>and</u>	*Connective of comparison*
the Himalayas have many more visitors now than a few years ago, brought about by the building of more roads to the areas.	*Explain: first link the two areas directly and compare what that means to each of them*
The visitors need places to stay and eat while they are there. For the Lake District, this means car parks, cafes and ice cream vans. <u>In contrast,</u>	*Use a connective of contrast to link the information in the two sentences*
the visitors to the Himalayas require trekking centres and base camps for climbing.	*Link the next sentence about rubbish to the previous one about food*
Food inevitably means that the tourists also need places to dispose of rubbish. <u>Furthermore,</u> in the Himalayas, climbers leave huge amounts of used equipment at the base camps.	*Use a connective of addition to show the problem in the Himalayas is actually worse*

Classworks Literacy Year 6 © Paula Ross, Nelson Thornes Ltd 2003

(Exemplar material)

Checklist for non-chronological reports

- Start with a clear opening paragraph that indicates what the report is about

- Include generalisations or classifications in the opening paragraph, for example, 'The Andes form one of the greatest mountain ranges in the world'

- Clearly organise the main body of the report into paragraphs or sections of linked information

- Make sure that the information is factual and accurate

- Order the report logically so it is easy to follow

- Use a formal style – personal pronouns are generally not used

- Use the present tense, unless writing historical reports

- Use precise, factual descriptive and technical language

- Can use subtitles (*for example, books such as those by Dorling Kindersley, where subtitles are common*)

- Use appropriate language to compare, contrast or classify (*it may be appropriate to add this on Day 7 when preparing a comparative report*)

- Write a summarising comment to finish the report

Marking ladder

Name: _____

Pupil	Objective	Teacher
	My report has a clear opening paragraph which indicates what it is about.	
	My opening paragraph includes generalisations or classifications.	
	The main body of my report is clearly organised into paragraphs (may be subtitled).	
	The information is factual and accurate.	
	The style is formal (no personal pronouns).	
	I used present tense.	
	I used precise descriptive language (technical terms).	
	I included a summarising comment to finish my report.	
	I used at least three complex sentences.	
	I used connectives of comparison and contrast in the 'Effect of tourists' section.	
	What could I do to improve my report next time?	

Discussion

Outcome

A written discussion paper and a class debate

Objectives

Sentence

3 to revise work on complex sentences: identifying main clauses; ways of connecting clauses; constructing complex sentences; appropriate use of punctuation.

5 to use reading to: investigate conditionals and their uses; use these forms to construct sentences which express, e.g. possibilities, hypotheses.

explore use of conditionals in past and future, experimenting with transformations, discussing effects, e.g. speculating about possible causes (past), reviewing a range of options and their outcomes (future).

Text

15 to recognise how arguments are constructed to be effective, through e.g.: the expression, sequence and linking of points; the provision of persuasive examples, illustrations and evidence; pre-empting or answering potential objections; appealing to the known views and feelings of the audience.

16 to identify the features of balanced written arguments which, e.g.: summarise different sides of an argument; clarify the strengths and weaknesses of different positions; signal personal opinion clearly.

18 to construct effective arguments: developing a point logically and effectively; supporting and illustrating points persuasively; anticipating possible objections; harnessing the known views, interests and feelings of the audience; tailoring the writing to formal presentation where appropriate.

19 to write a balanced report of a controversial issue: summarising fairly the competing views; analysing strengths and weaknesses of different positions.

Planning frame

- Read, analyse and annotate features of balanced discussion.
- Investigate planning frames, research and write a balanced report.
- Read, analyse and annotate features of a persuasive argument.
- Write a persuasive argument.
- Present a persuasive argument through class debate.

How you could plan this unit

Day 1	Day 2	Day 3	Day 4	Day 5
Reading and analysis Analyse two pieces of writing. Collect linking words and phrases. Build checklist	**Modelling and writing** Fast planning from the texts used on Day 1. (The DfES Planning Exemplification 2 provides good reading and analysis material for days 1 and 2)	**Modelling and planning** *Planning an Argument*	**Modelling and writing** *Writing an Argument*	**Modelling and writing** *Concluding an Argument*

Day 6	Day 7	Day 8	Day 9	Day 10
Reading, annotating and analysis *Persuasive Writing*	**Modelling and writing** Use the examples plus checklist to analyse the structure and produce a planning strategy	**Research, modelling and writing** *Class Debate*	**Planning, writing, speaking and listening** Appoint speakers, add the connectives which move one point to another. Rehearse presentations and prepare possible questions	**Speaking and listening** Discuss speaking for different audiences. Conventions of debating. Consider ways of handling disagreement constructively. Hold class debate

Planning an Argument

Objectives

We will collect and organise ideas for a balanced argument.
We will also familiarise ourselves with possible planning frames
for a discussion

You need: Resource Pages A (class set and display version), B and I; scissors; paper; glue.

Whole class work

- *School uniform has been worn in the UK for hundreds of years. In America they are just starting to introduce it. The focus of our work today is to collect and sort views into those for and those against, and to organise a plan for writing an argument.*

- Read the school uniform poster (Resource Page A). Divide the board into two columns headed 'For' and 'Against'. Select the argument *"You can't tell the difference between the haves and the have-nots"* – a positive effect of uniform for pupils who might have felt uncomfortable going to school because their family could not afford designer labels and they were teased because of it. Write it under 'For'.

- Select *"The cost of clothes for school can be very expensive."* You could interpret this statement in two ways – school uniform could be expensive or own clothes could be expensive. Everyone has to buy ordinary clothes, so buying a school uniform as well would be expensive or children would want to wear stylish clothes to school that may not be very hardwearing. Write this in the centre of the board.

- Review the checklist for what a balanced argument needs (Resource Page I). Emphasise the idea of giving reasons for a point of view.

- Draw or display the two planning frames (Resource Page B). Explain the difference between them.

- In order to write an effective argument, we need to link together similar statements to write in the same paragraph. *Can you find some statements from the resource sheet that can be linked together?*

- Ask the children for suggestions for the question title for their balanced argument. Select an appropriate one, for example: "Should pupils be made to wear school uniform?"

Independent, pair or guided work

- The children write the question title and divide their page into two sections titled 'For' and 'Against'. Then they cut up the speech bubbles, organise similar arguments together and glue them in their books under the appropriate headings, or centrally if it fits both arguments.

- They could add arguments of their own in the empty speech bubbles.

Plenary

- In pairs, one child selects a statement in favour of school uniform and gives their reasons, the other gives a counter-argument with reasons. Then reverse the roles.

- One or two pairs present their ideas to the class. *Do their arguments give a balanced view (one for, one against)? Can they give reasons for their argument?*

Writing an Argument

Objectives

We will write an introductory paragraph. We will then use our organised ideas to write a balanced argument

You need: Resource Pages B–D and I; a child's organised statements from previous lesson.

Whole class work	• Review the features of a balanced argument. Check the offered suggestions against the checklist (Resource Page I). Then display the checklist, making reference to it throughout.
	• Model writing the first paragraph, ensuring you: – include facts/statistics – explain what the argument is about – use a degree of formality, for example, passive voice, formal language – include at least one connective – keep the views impersonal – use the language of debate.
Independent, pair or guided work	• The children write their own first paragraph. Some children might wish to use your modelled work, substituting the "Some people believe ..." sentence for one of their own.
Whole class work	• Refer to the planning frames from the previous lesson (Resource Page B) and ask the children to decide which format they intend to use: all the arguments for, all the arguments against, or argument and counter-argument.
	• Ask the children to look at their organised statements from the previous lesson. Explain that they should select from all the reasons the ones that they think are the most important. Remind them that they could link one or two of the ideas together but they must give reasons to substantiate the views.
	• Emphasise the need to see the argument from both sides even though they may have a personal opinion.
	• Model how to write an argument and counter-argument using connectives to give a balanced view (see Resource Pages C and D).
Independent, pair or guided work	• The children start to write their arguments and counter arguments. This activity will run into the next lesson.
Plenary	• In pairs, the children read each other's work and comment critically. The children should identify a well-structured sentence and give reasons why it works, mentioning any points from the checklist that have been used. They should also find a sentence where they can offer suggestions for improvement.

Concluding an Argument

Objectives

We will continue to use our organised ideas to write our balanced argument. We will write a conclusion to the argument, and then assess our work using a marking ladder

You need: Resource Pages D, I and J.

Whole class work

- Using checklist 1 (Resource Page I), discuss what a concluding paragraph needs. Brainstorm ideas from the class.

- Model a concluding paragraph (Resource Page D).

- Hand out the marking ladder (Resource Page J). Go through the features and ask the children to review their work so far to see if they need to edit in order to ensure they include all the features.

Independent, pair or guided work

- Complete the body of the text.

- Write a concluding paragraph.

Plenary

- Read out features from the marking ladder. Ask the children to locate the feature in their text and tick the child's section of the marking ladder.

- Ask the children to highlight/underline/write in the margin particular features. This makes your own assessment easier and also gives a clear indication whether the pupil has understood the feature.

Persuasive Writing

Objective

We will read, analyse and annotate persuasive arguments

You need: Resource Pages E–G and I; large sheet of paper for checklist.

Whole class work

- *Not all arguments give a balanced view. Some are written from only a pro or anti viewpoint and are designed to persuade the reader to agree with the writer – like a pamphlet from an environmental group or a political party.*

- Read the piece on school camps (Resource Page E). Together, analyse and annotate the text to find the main features (see Resource Page F).

- Add the features to a class checklist for persuasive argument (see Resource Page I for ideas).

Independent, pair or guided work

- Ask the children to read the information sheet about smoking (Resource Page G). They should highlight any points that promote the view that smoking is dangerous for young people, and annotate which features of persuasive argument they show.

Plenary

- Call out points from the checklist, and ask the children for examples from the text.

- Decide whether other points need to be added to the checklist.

Class Debate

Objectives

We will research the agreed argument for class debate. We will plan the points for the argument and supporting evidence. Finally we will prioritise them

You need: Resource Pages A, H and I; strips of paper for brainstorming.

Whole class work

- Remind the children of the balanced argument written about school uniform. ***How would that argument differ if it were a persuasive argument?*** Answer: it gives both points of view whereas a persuasive argument gives the views of the pro- *or* the anti-school uniform group.

- Tell the children that they are going to prepare their arguments for a class debate to be held the following day. Explain the rudiments of debating:

  > DEBATING – THE BASICS
  >
  > Chair introduces the subject to be debated
  >
  > A representative(s) of the For motion introduces and gives their views
  >
  > Followed by a representative(s) of the Against group
  >
  > The For group concludes and the Against group concludes
  >
  > This could be followed by a question time from the floor before a vote is taken

- Using a display version of the school uniform poster (Resource Page A), ask for examples a pro-uniform group would use and those an anti-uniform group would use.

- Model how to present the anti group's ideas, referring to Resource Pages H and I.

- Explain that in a debate it is also necessary to predict the argument your opponents might give and be ready to counter their views.

Independent, pair or guided work

- Divide the class into two mixed-ability groups, one pro, the other anti. Appoint a Chair and Secretary for each group.

- Allow the children to suggest a subject for debate or suggest: "Celebrities should be required to teach one day a week in a school." Explain that celebrities are often talented people who earn huge salaries – in order to earn their salaries they should be required to pass on their skills to the younger generation, for example, sports players teach PE lessons, chefs give cookery lessons and so on.

- The Chair and Secretary work on the introduction to the debate, while (initially in pairs), the rest of the group brainstorm possible arguments. The pairs report back to the Chair and Secretary who write the collated ideas on to strips of paper.

- The group spends a few minutes organising points into a priority order, removing weaker points or linking similar ones together. In pairs or small groups, the children write a persuasive paragraph about one of the points using the planning frame.

Plenary

- The pairs read their argument to the rest of the group who give editing ideas.

- The Chair then decides in which order the points should be presented.

(**Pupil copymaster**)

School uniform v own clothes – a poster

Gang identification is harder.

It makes it easier to identify children out of school.

It keeps the focus on learning and not fashion.

The cost of clothes for school can be very expensive.

My Nike trainers were stolen.

Designer labels are cool.

You can't tell the difference between the haves and the have-nots.

Everyone looks the same.

It inspires a feeling of belonging – like when I wear the school football kit.

Strangers are easily detected.

It cuts down on the time I need to decide what to wear.

My clothes show my creativeness.

Individuals develop through their personality and skills not their appearance.

Where is the freedom to choose?

I feel more confident in my own clothes.

I feel safe.

When dressed neatly and seriously, students tend to behave seriously.

I'm always late because I have to find my school jumper and I can't just put on any jumper.

Classworks Literacy Year 6 © Paula Ross, Nelson Thornes Ltd 2003

127

(Pupil copymaster)

Two planning frames

A question for the title

Introduction
- *gives facts / statistics*
- *explains what the argument is about*

Arguments For
- *reasons to support the argument*

Arguments Against
- *sums up and may offer suggestions*

Conclusion

Title

Introduction

Statement 1
Reasons for and against

Statement 2
Reasons for and against

Statement 3
Reasons for and against

Conclusion

(Exemplar material)

Examples of modelling a balanced argument

Introductory paragraph

Write this on the board...	...while you are saying this
Should children be made to wear school uniform?	**First paragraph will state why the title question is being discussed.**
Most	*Start with a fact. Try to give numerical data if possible.*
pupils in the United Kingdom wear a	*Present tense.*
school uniform. It is a tradition dating back to Tudor times. In contrast,	*Connective to give the other view.*
President Clinton of the USA in 1996 encouraged parents, pupils and governors to adopt school uniform for the first time. Some people believe	*Don't put personal opinions. Use language of debate.*
that school uniform helps provide a positive and creative way to reduce discipline problems and increase school safety.	*Now need a sentence to bring the two ideas together and launch into the arguments.*
Considerable debate	*Language of debate.*
has taken place	*Passive voice for formality.*
over many years as to whether school uniform is a tradition which has had its day.	*Reader has a clear indication of what the argument will be about.*

Body text

	Select the points to make in the first argument: • *clothes become a focus instead of work evidence* • *children's love of 'labels'.* *Counter-argument:* • *clothes don't distract other pupils – haven't heard pupils complaining that they can't work because of clothes.*

Continued ...

(Exemplar material)

Examples of modelling a balanced argument (continued)

	First argument – start a new paragraph – indent.
Supporters of school uniform	*Use ways to introduce views that are impersonal.*
believe	*Language of debate and present tense.*
that normal clothes might	*Use conditionals.*
be distracting to someone's studies and that the clothing takes away	*Present tense.*
from the importance of why the pupil is in school.	*Main focus of the argument.*
They state that pupils are more interested in the labels on the clothes than their work.	*Argument backed up with evidence.*
On the other hand,	*Connective to give a balanced view.*
many people would argue that pupils do not wear clothes with the intention of distracting other pupils	*Main focus of the argument.*
and would back this up	*Backed up with evidence.*
by asking if anyone has heard pupils complain they are unable to do their work because someone's shirt is too bright.	

Concluding paragraph

	Final paragraph needs to sum up the arguments and provide a suggestion of what might happen. New paragraph – indent.
While there are clearly many reasons why school uniform *might*	*Conditional.*
be disliked by pupils, there are also many reasons why schools *should*	
have a school uniform.	*Sentence gives points of view of the pupils and the school.*
Maybe, though, it is time to provide a uniform which, while hard-wearing and smart, does appeal more to the pupils	*Suggestion which incorporates both sides of the argument.*
In my opinion, it is time to provide a uniform that while hard-wearing and smart, does appeal more to the pupils.	*Alternative end sentence. Explain to pupils that it is permissible to write their own opinion in the final paragraph but they must give a reason for what they decide or suggest.*

(**Pupil copymaster**)

School camps should be banned

School camps should be banned. In the last five years society has become much more aware of the problems of school camps. Reports in the media have shown that the activities might be dangerous. Outdoor centres often provide poor food and accommodation and most importantly children attending camp waste valuable lesson time. The Government should reassess the value of sending primary school children on outdoor and adventurous activities at residential camps.

Firstly, children are required to sleep in dormitories or tents with many others. Do the organisers not realise that children can fall out with just one brother or sister sharing their bedroom? Eight others in the room is a disaster. Either World War III breaks out or it is treated as a giant sleepover with children awake until three and four in the morning.

Furthermore, many of the activities undertaken are competitive. This simply encourages the children to become big-headed. Their lack of maturity means that many spend the week boasting of their achievements while the teacher's self-esteem reaches rock bottom when the pupils constantly remind them of their walking round rather than climbing over the wall in the obstacle course.

Finally, the equipment for the activities. Pulling children into and out of damp wetsuits is a dangerous occupation for any teacher, resulting in pulled muscles and the consequent inability to write on the board when the party return to school. Moreover, being chased and then tipped out of a canoe by a vicious mob of year 6 pupils is the last straw.

In conclusion, it is evident that school camp is a very hazardous aspect of the teacher's job and should be removed from their list of duties. Not only does it reduce the teacher to a quivering wreck with low self-esteem, tired beyond belief, never wanting to see another chip, but it also produces highly excited and animated children who waste valuable lesson time talking about when they can go again.

(Exemplar analysis)

Example of analysis of *School camps should be banned*

Ask: whose viewpoint is written in this argument? Answer: teacher's.

Title is a statement that can be agreed with or opposed.

Passive voice makes it sound formal and important (examples in italics).

Impersonal (examples underlined in grey).

Use of the conditional means it is not definite.

Structural connective.

Rhetorical question and also a "dare you disagree with me?".

Connective to introduce another argument ...

... followed by details to elaborate the point of view.

Structural connective, with a subtitle used like a sentence.

Structural connective.

First paragraph states a point of view. Following paragraphs back it up with detailed evidence.

Opinion – examples underlined.

Emotive language.

Present tense (examples in bold).

Further argument ... connecting the argument to its – elaboration.

Emotive language.

Return to the main viewpoint of the argument.

Final paragraph sums up the argument.

School camps should be banned. In the last five years society *has become* much more aware of the problems of school camps. Reports in the media *have shown* that the activities might be dangerous. Outdoor centres often provide poor food and accommodation and most importantly children attending camp waste valuable lesson time. The Government should reassess the value of sending primary school children on outdoor and adventurous activities at residential camps.

Firstly, children *are required* to sleep in dormitories or tents with many others. Do the organisers not realise that children can fall out with just one brother or sister sharing their bedroom? Eight others in the room is a disaster. Either World War III breaks out or it is treated as a giant sleepover with children awake until three and four in the morning.

Furthermore, many of the activities undertaken are competitive. This simply **encourages** the children to become big-headed. Their lack of maturity **means** that many spend the week boasting of their achievements whilst the teacher's self-esteem **reaches** rock bottom when the pupils constantly **remind** them of their walking round rather than climbing over the wall in the obstacle course.

Finally, the equipment for the activities. Pulling children into and out of damp wetsuits is a dangerous occupation for any teacher, resulting in pulled muscles and the consequent inability to write on the board when the party return to school. Moreover, being chased and then tipped out of a canoe by a vicious mob of year 6 pupils is the last straw.

In conclusion, it is evident that school camp is a very hazardous aspect of the teacher's job and should be removed from their list of duties. Not only does it reduce the teacher to a quivering wreck with low self-esteem, tired beyond belief, never wanting to see another chip, but it also produces highly excited and animated children who waste valuable lesson time talking about when they can go again.

(Pupil copymaster)

Ban the tobacco industry from encouraging children to smoke

Did you know that tobacco companies in the USA spend a record $26 million a day to market their deadly products? In the United States, 12–17 year olds smoke more than 900 million packs of cigarettes per year. One in three will die prematurely. It's outrageous! The big tobacco companies are to blame.

In the first place, tobacco is probably the most dangerous substance commonly consumed by humans. Teenagers smoke for a variety of reasons but wanting to be 'cool' is the reason the tobacco companies use most often in their advertising. The brands of cigarettes that teenagers prefer in America are Marlboro, Camel and Newport, the three most heavily advertised. Several studies found that the leading cigarette brands all increased their advertising in music and fashion magazines bought mainly by teenagers.

Secondly, the companies look for gimmicks to entice teenagers. Trendy tin boxes are the latest marketing ploy to lure young smokers. The tin boxes hold a packet of cigarettes to prevent them from being crushed in a pocket or handbag. But the fashionable tin boxes also hide the health warnings on the side of the packets.

The tobacco companies are making millions in profits from sales to these kids. At the same time, effective regulations to help reduce youth smoking are often blocked because of the millions of dollars that the tobacco companies spend every year on contributions to governments.

As a consequence of the actions of these tobacco companies, cigarette-related illnesses kill more than 400,000 Americans every year – more deaths than from AIDS, alcohol, car accidents, murders, suicides, drugs and fires, combined. Nearly every adult who smokes took his or her first puff at or before the age of 18. It appears that tobacco company profits are more important than children's lives. The companies should be made to stop using advertising and gimmicks aimed at encouraging children to smoke.

State arguments to support the point of view and elaborate each one.

Classworks Literacy Year 6 © Paula Ross, Nelson Thornes Ltd 2003

(Exemplar material)

'School uniform should be banned' – modelling the counter-argument for a debate

Write this on the board ...	... while you are saying this
School uniform should be banned	*Title becomes a statement that one group can agree with and one group disagree with.*
Mr / Madam Chairman, ladies and gentlemen,	*Formal introduction to the debate.*
we would like to counter the proposition	*Language of debate.*
that school uniform should be banned.	*State their view.*
In our opinion school uniform is an important part of belonging to our school	*Back up the view with a very important general reason ...*
and we offer the following arguments for ensuring that it continues to be part of our school.	*... and state what you are going to do next.*
Firstly,	*Structural connective.*
school uniform is a very practical way of dressing for school.	*State the point.*
The clothes are made from hard-wearing materials that can be washed easily, a necessary requirement for all the activities pupils undertake in a week and a bonus if every playtime is spent playing football. In addition,	*Then back it up with further details.* *Connective to add an extra linked point.*
school uniform can be bought in many stores	*Another practicality.*
at reasonable prices so it is easy for parents to find and afford.	*Giving the listener food for thought – implying that ordinary clothes are not practical, cost a lot of money and parents will have to shop in specialist stores. Continue by talking through the other points which this group might make, for example, sense of belonging, pupils concentrate on work not fashion and so on.*

(Exemplar material)

Checklists for writing arguments

Example of a checklist for writing a balanced argument

- Use a question for the title
- Give facts/statistics in the introduction and explain what the argument is about
- Give statements for and against with reasons to support
- Use the final paragraph to sum up and possibly to offer suggestions
- The final paragraph may include an opinion
- Use language of debate, for example, 'no-one can deny', 'some people believe'
- Use verbs mainly in the present tense
- Include examples of the passive
- Use conditionals: 'would', 'could', 'might'
- Use impersonal pronouns
- Use connectives to:
  - introduce more points: 'furthermore'
  - give a balanced view: 'however'
  - draw to a conclusion: 'consequently'

Example of a checklist for writing a persuasive argument

- Make the introduction a statement giving a point of view
- Give arguments to support the point of view
- State and clearly explain each argument
- In the summary state the point of view again
- Use persuasive devices, for example:
  - statistics
  - emotive language: strong adjectives
  - rhetorical questions: 'Are we to believe that …'
  - deliberate ambiguity:'possibly', 'probably'
- Ensure that opinions are supported and sound like facts
- Use mainly present tense
- Include examples of conditionals – 'would', 'could', 'might'
- Introduce each argument with a structural connective – 'Firstly'
- Use logical connectives – 'so'/'therefore' – to link ideas within arguments

(Marking ladder)

Marking ladder for a balanced argument

Name: _____

Pupil	Objective	Teacher
	I used a question for the title.	
	My introduction explains what the argument is about.	
	I gave statements for and against, with reasons to support them.	
	My final paragraph sums up and may offer suggestions.	
	I used three examples of the language of debate, for example, 'no-one can deny', 'some people believe': 1) 2) 3)	
	I used verbs: • mainly in the present tense • including examples of the passive • including conditionals, e.g. 'would', 'could', 'might'.	
	I used impersonal pronouns (third person): 'it', 'they'.	
	I used a personal pronoun in the final paragraph only (optional).	
	I used connectives that: • introduce more points: 'furthermore' • give a balanced view: 'however' • draw to a conclusion: 'consequently'.	
	What could I do to improve my balanced argument next time?	

Classworks Literacy Year 6 © Paula Ross, Nelson Thornes Ltd 2003

Marking ladder

Marking ladder for a persuasive argument

Name: _____

Pupil	Objective	Teacher
	I stated my point of view clearly in the introduction and in the conclusion.	
	I backed up each argument with relevant evidence and detail.	
	My argument is mainly in the present tense.	
	I used conditionals.	
	I used connectives: • to structure the argument: 'first', 'finally'. • to link ideas within the argument: 'because', consequently'.	
	I used persuasive devices such as: • statistics • emotive language • rhetorical questions.	
	What could I do to make my writing more persuasive next time?	

Formal Writing

Outcome

A leaflet giving safety guidance about children's use of technology; a formal letter to headteachers about the leaflet

Objectives

Sentence

2 to understand features of formal official language through, e.g.:
- collecting and analysing examples, discussing when and why they are used;
- noting the conventions of the language, e.g. use of impersonal voice, imperative verbs, formal vocabulary;
- collecting typical words and expressions e.g. 'those wishing to', 'hereby', 'forms may be obtained'.

3 to revise work on complex sentences: identifying main clauses; ways of connecting clauses; constructing complex sentences; appropriate use of punctuation.

4 to revise work on contracting sentences: summary; note-making; editing.

Text

17 to read and understand examples of official language and its characteristic features, e.g. through discussing consumer information, legal documents, layouts, use of footnotes, instructions, parentheses, headings, appendices and asterisks.

20 to discuss the way standard English varies in different contexts, e.g. why legal language is necessarily highly formalised, why questionnaires must be specific.

Planning frame

- Analyse formally written fact sheets and leaflets: use of imperative, complex sentences.
- Write and design (ICT) leaflet on the dangers of technology for children.

How you could plan this unit

Day 1	Day 2	Day 3	Day 4	Day 5
Reading and analysis	Modelling and presenting information	Reading and analysis Texts analysed and annotated: safety using computers and Internet	Reading and analysis Make notes from the texts presented this week	Model planning and writing
Common Features	*Interpreting Texts*			*Producing a Leaflet*

Day 6	Day 7	Day 8	Day 9	Day 10
Modelling and writing Produce an official leaflet incorporating features of formal writing	Modelling and writing Continue writing official leaflet	Reading and analysis	Modelling and writing	Writing Produce and assess an official leaflet. Completion of leaflet and marking ladder
		Formal Letters	*Letter Writing*	

Common Features

Objectives

We will identify the features of official writing and understand the information in an official document. We will start a class collection of official words and phrases

You need: Resource Pages A–F and N; display paper.

Whole class work

- Explain that formal language is used in a variety of documents, for example, public information documents, solicitors' letters, police reports, rules (safety at swimming pools, and so on), enquiries, complaints.

- Ask the children to find examples of official documents in the classroom (evacuation/fire drill procedures, rules for using the Internet, code of conduct).

- Explain that the outcome of the work about formal writing will be to produce a leaflet giving safety guidance about children's use of technology, in particular computers, the Internet and mobile phones. They will also write a formal letter to headteachers to explain the launch of their safety leaflet.

- Read the text on mobile phones and driving (Resource Page A).

- Model analysing and annotating the text (Resource Page B), emphasising the importance of language selection in order to write formally, specifically:

> the use of standard English for clarity and to ensure there are no ambiguities
>
> the use of a technical and formal vocabulary
>
> the need for a studied politeness and yet forceful way of writing
> (often provided by the use of the imperative voice)

- Explain that because formal writing can be used in a huge range of texts, there are few generic text features but there are many sentence and word features. As the children study various formal texts, they may find text-linked features, for example, a letter may have a subtitle 'Re: ...' to inform the reader about the subject of the letter.

- Start a class collection of official language used in the sample text.

- Leave Resource Page B on display.

Independent, pair or guided work

- Show the children the safety leaflet (Resource Pages C and D). Explain that this is a formal document giving advice about the use of mobile phones when driving. (It was distributed to all employees of Cornwall County Council.)

- Using Resource Page B for reference, the children analyse and annotate features that show formal writing has been used (see Resource Pages E and F).

Plenary

- ***What indicators of formal writing have you noticed?*** Add suggestions to a class checklist for formal writing (see Resource Page N for ideas).

- Refer back to the text to find any other features.

Interpreting Texts

Objective

We will transcribe formal writing into an informal presentation, shortening sentences by identifying key points

You need: Resource Pages I and J.

Whole class work

- Tell the children that they will meet many examples of formal writing in life and it is important that they can understand and interpret the texts. Although standard English is generally used, it does not mean it will be simple or straightforward language.

- *The lesson today will teach you how to understand a formal document and how to make an informal presentation of the material.*

- Read Resource Page I on texting and explain it comes from a web site set up for parents to help them to keep their children safe when they are using technology.

- *Your task is to present the information in pictorial form with a few notes where required for adults who have difficulty in reading English.*

- Model transcribing the information (Resource Page J).

Independent, pair or guided work

- The children select two of the other sections – security risks, safety risks, exploitation risks or costs – and transcribe the formal text into a pictorial presentation.

Plenary

- The children display their work on table tops. Ask them to view all the work and stand by the drawings that in their opinion best represent:
  - security risks
  - safety risks
  - exploitation risks
  - costs.

- *Why have you selected this representation?*

Producing a Leaflet

Objectives

We will plan and produce a safety leaflet for parents about children's use of technology. We will take care to write formally, using features from the checklist

You need: Resource Pages A, C–H and N; computers and DTP software (optional).

Whole class work

- Remind the children of the outcome of this block of work – a safety leaflet for parents giving advice about children's use of technology.

- Tell the children that the mobile phone leaflet (Resource Pages C and D) was produced by a road safety unit that is part of a county council. **Who are you representing as writers of the technology safety leaflet?** Answer: teachers/the school.

- **What aspects of technology could be included in the leaflet?** Answer: use of computers, Internet and mobile phones.

- Review the original text for this unit (Resource Page A) and remind the children of the features they annotated on the leaflet (Resource Pages E and F). Mention:
  - use of subtitles to divide the sections
  - highlighting key information as separate facts in ways that attract the reader
  - illustrations to break up text and reinforce messages
  - use of colour and different-sized fonts for emphasis.

- Using a template, model how the leaflet could be organised (Resource Page G) and how part of it could be analysed (Resource Page H).

- Model writing the introductory section, showing the children how to use questions to make the reader think, grab their attention and make them want to find out more. Refer to the checklist (Resource Page N) and ask the children to note which features you have included:

● imperative verbs	● technical vocabulary
● stilted politeness	● complex sentences
● conditionals	● standard English to be exact and clear with no ambiguities

Independent, pair or guided work

- Referring to the modelled versions, the children brainstorm section headings and general layout for their leaflet. (You may want to distribute leaflet templates or use DTP software to support this activity.)

- The children write their introductory section.

Plenary

- Refer back to the checklist. The children note how may of the features they have included in their first section.

- Ask them to feed back specific examples from the checklist, for example, technical language, use of conditionals and so on.

- Ask the class to comment on their effectiveness using a response sandwich for evaluation: one positive comment, one area for improvement, another positive comment.

Formal Letters

Objective

We will read and analyse formal letters and identify their main features

You need: Resource Pages K, L and N; display paper.

Whole class work

- Explain that having prepared their safety leaflet, the children need to distribute it to as many parents as possible, for example, by pupil post in school. (Has there been a recent occasion when the children did this, for example, meningitis information from a local health authority?)

- In order to do this, the children need to write to the headteacher to explain:

> who they are
>
> their reason for writing
>
> what the leaflet is about
>
> what they want the headteacher to do

- *Would this letter be a formal or informal one? Why?* Point out that formal letters are usually written to someone you do not know.

- *In today's lesson you will look at some examples of formal letters and establish a checklist of features that you can use when writing your own letter tomorrow.*

- Read Resource Page K. Model analysing the text and annotate the features, pointing out the sections where the sender explains who he is, his reason for writing, gives more details about the problems and explains what he wants the education authority to do.

- *Many of the features annotated previously when looking at formal texts are present in letters as well.*

- Ask for examples of situations when a formal letter might be written. Answer: a complaint, enquiry about holiday accommodation, request for a bank loan, information from or to the council.

Independent, pair or guided work

- Display Resource Page K while the children analyse and annotate another sample letter (Resource Page L).

Plenary

- Through re-examining Resource Page K and their own letter, the children offer suggestions for a checklist of features (see Resource Page N for ideas). Scribe their suggestions on to display paper.

Letter Writing

Objective

We will write a formal letter incorporating the layout and features established in the checklist

You need: Resource Pages M and N.

Whole class work	• Review the features of a formal letter from the previous lesson. • Establish what needs to be written in the sections of the letter:

> <u>Who the senders are</u> — refer back to the lesson when the class decided which group of people they were representing as writers of the leaflet.
>
> <u>Their reason for writing</u> — to inform as many parents as possible how to keep their children safe when using technology.
>
> <u>What the leaflet is about</u> — hazards of the Internet, computers in general and mobile phones and how to overcome them (some specific examples could be included). It may be useful to tell the headteacher that many of the safety suggestions are pertinent to schools as well as homes.
>
> <u>What they want the headteacher to do</u> — distribute the leaflets to the children to take home.

• Through suggestions from the class, scribe the layout of the addresses for the letter.

• Model writing the first paragraph (Resource Page M) describing who you are and the reason for writing.

Independent, pair or guided work	• The children write their letter to the headteacher.

Plenary	• Refer to the checklist (Resource Page N) as the children highlight, underline or use colour to demonstrate where they have included various features in their letters.

(Pupil copymaster)

Fact sheet

MOBILE PHONES and DRIVING

INTRODUCTION

Mobile phones provide a range of benefits and are extremely popular. However, many drivers use them to make and receive calls, or to send and receive text messages, while they are driving. Drivers need 100 per cent of their attention on driving 100 per cent of the time. Traffic situations constantly change and an accident can easily happen in seconds. Therefore, anything that has the potential to distract the driver should be avoided.

Using a mobile phone while driving is a significant physical and cognitive distraction and increases the risk of the driver being involved in an accident.

RoSPA POLICY

No driver should use a mobile telephone or any similar piece of telecommunications equipment (whether hand-held or hands free) while driving.

Such use is likely to distract the driver from the main task of managing the vehicle in a safe and competent manner and be prejudicial to road safety. Calls should not be made or received while on the move. Ideally, an interlock should be integral in all such equipment so that it is rendered inoperable while the vehicle is moving. Where this is not possible, it is recommended that all telecommunications equipment is switched off while the driver is driving.

Employers are recommended to incorporate this policy within their own rules governing company drivers. Vehicles are intended to transport their occupants and goods to their destination(s) and any temptation to turn vehicles into 'mobile offices' should be resisted.

THE LAW

The Highway Code now specifically warns drivers that they MUST be in proper control of their vehicle at all times, and strongly advises drivers not to use mobile phones (and other equipment) while driving. See page 32, sections 127 and 128 (and 126 for other distractions).

Regulation 104 of the Construction and Use Regulations indicates that drivers may face prosecution if they are not at all times in proper control of their vehicle. This regulation has already been used as the basis for prosecution by police officers nationwide.

Royal Society for the Prevention of Accidents (abridged)

(Exemplar analysis)

Example of analysis of fact sheet

Adversative connective –
shows a contrasting view
is about to be expressed.

Complex
sentence.

Conditional
statement.

Subtitles for
clarity. This
is an official
document
from road
safety
organisation.

Impersonal.

Passive voice
for formality.

Formal tone.

Use of
technical
terms.

Causal
connective
forms a link
between the
cause and
the effect.

Use of
standard
English to
give clear
and exact
information
without
ambiguities.

Formal
vocabulary
(underlined).

Complex
sentence.

Information
in bold
carries more
authority.

MOBILE PHONES and DRIVING

INTRODUCTION

Mobile phones provide a range of benefits and are extremely popular. However, many drivers use them to make and receive calls, or to send and receive text messages, while they are driving. Drivers need 100 per cent of their attention on driving 100 per cent of the time. Traffic situations constantly change and an accident can easily happen in seconds. Therefore, anything that has the potential to distract the driver should be avoided.

Using a mobile phone while driving is a significant physical and cognitive distraction and increases the risk of the driver being involved in an accident.

RoSPA POLICY

No driver should use a mobile telephone or any similar piece of telecommunications equipment (whether hand-held or hands free) while driving.

Such use is likely to distract the driver from the main task of <u>managing the vehicle</u> in a <u>safe and competent manner</u> and be <u>prejudicial to road safety</u>. Calls should not be made or received while on the move. Ideally, an interlock should be integral in all such equipment so that it is <u>rendered inoperable</u> while the vehicle is moving. Where this is not possible, it is recommended that all telecommunications equipment is switched off while the driver is driving.

Employers <u>are recommended</u> to <u>incorporate this policy</u> within their own rules governing company drivers. Vehicles are intended to transport their occupants and goods to their destination(s) and any temptation to turn vehicles into 'mobile offices' should be resisted.

THE LAW

The Highway Code now specifically warns drivers that they MUST be in <u>proper control</u> of their vehicle at all times, and strongly advises drivers not to use mobile phones (and other equipment) while driving. See page 32, sections 127 and 128 (and 126 for other distractions).

Regulation 104 of the Construction and Use Regulations indicates that drivers may face prosecution if they are not at all times in proper control of their vehicle. This regulation has already been used as the basis for prosecution by police officers nationwide.

Royal Society for the Prevention of Accidents (abridged)

Use of parentheses
(brackets) to enclose
statements that give
extra information
and are independent
of rest of sentence.

There is a politeness about
the whole document yet it
also sounds official and
gives weighty information to
the reader.

(**Pupil copymaster**)

Mobile phones and driving leaflet

THE LAW

You **MUST** exercise proper control of your vehicle at **ALL** times.

Never use a hand held mobile phone or microphone when driving. Using hands free equipment is also likely to distract your attention from the road.

It is **safer not to** use any telephone while you are driving - find a safe place to stop first.

The penalties include:
An unlimited fine
Disqualification and
Up to two years imprisonment

(Law RTA 1988 Sections 2 and 3)

THE FACTS

Mobile phones have been implicated in at least 17 deaths on Britain's roads, but there have been many more - likely thousands of accidents have taken place because of mobiles.

Using a mobile telephone makes accidents four times more likely.

Source - ROSPA

Classworks Literacy Year 6 © Paula Ross, Nelson Thornes Ltd 2003

Pupil copymaster

Leaflet (continued)

EMPLOYEES

Driving and using a mobile phone are both demanding tasks that should not be carried out at the same time.

Responsibility for the safe control of a vehicle always rests with the driver. The law clearly states that you must have proper control of your vehicle.

If it is essential for you to be contacted while you are driving, use voicemail or call diversion and stop regularly to check messages and return calls.

If hands-free equipment is used, it should be installed according to the manufacturers' instructions and should follow the British Standards Institution's "Guide to in-vehicle information systems".

(DD 235: 1996)

It can also be an offence for employers to require their employees to use mobile phones while driving.

Do not use a mobile phone close to a vehicle carrying flammable loads.

Driving today requires all of your attention all of the time

Never use a hand-held phone while driving

It is safer not to use a hands-free phone while driving

Use a message service and take regular breaks

Road Safety

DRIVER RESPONSIBILITY

Regardless of how competent a driver claims to be, no-one can hold a phone, obtain a number, conduct a conversation and be in complete control of their vehicle. It is simply not the same as having a conversation with a passenger or listening to a tape or the radio.

It takes less than a split second for a lapse in concentration to result in an accident.

Drivers behaving in this way endanger the safety of the public generally and their own safety too.

THE ADVICE

✔ The only **safe way** for drivers to use a mobile phone in a vehicle is when they have stopped in a safe place.

✘ **Don't** distract yourself by using a mobile phone, reading a map or business documents, eating or drinking while driving.

✘ **Never** use a hand held phone while driving.

✘ **Do not** fix a mobile phone to the dashboard, in a position where an inflating airbag could dislodge it and push it in your face.

✘ **Do not** use a mobile phone if there is a danger from petrol spillage or fumes.

Classworks Literacy Year 6 © Paula Ross, Nelson Thornes Ltd 2003

(Exemplar analysis)

Example of analysis of mobile phones and driving leaflet

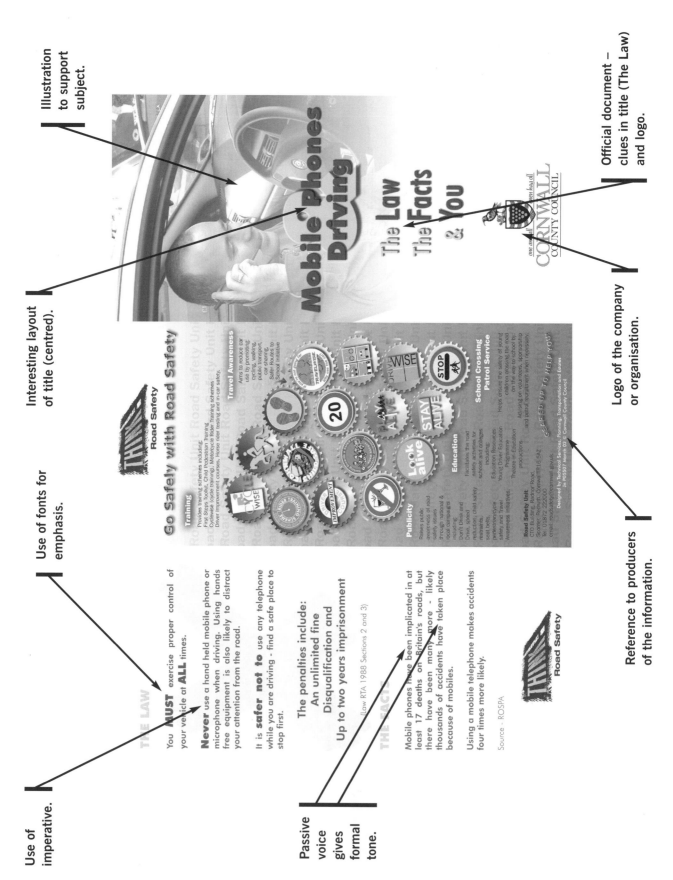

Illustration to support subject.

Official document – clues in title (The Law) and logo.

Interesting layout of title (centred).

Logo of the company or organisation.

Use of fonts for emphasis.

Reference to producers of the information.

Use of imperative.

Passive voice gives formal tone.

(Exemplar analysis)

Analysis of leaflet (continued)

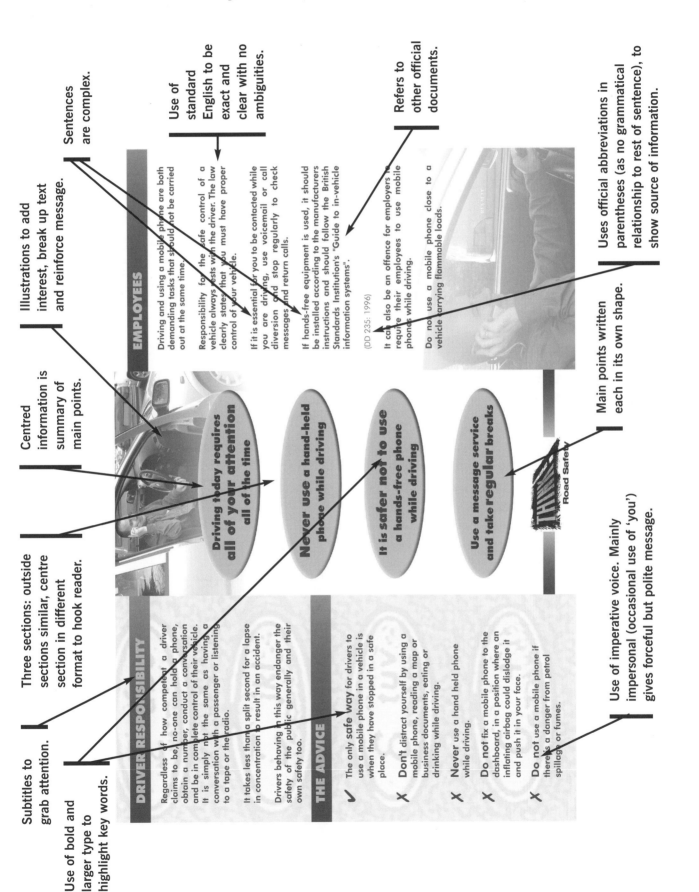

Annotations:

Sentences are complex.

Use of standard English to be exact and clear with no ambiguities.

Refers to other official documents.

Uses official abbreviations in parentheses (as no grammatical relationship to rest of sentence), to show source of information.

Illustrations to add interest, break up text and reinforce message.

Centred information is summary of main points.

Three sections: outside sections similar, centre section in different format to hook reader.

Subtitles to grab attention.

Use of bold and larger type to highlight key words.

Main points written each in its own shape.

Use of imperative voice. Mainly impersonal (occasional use of 'you') gives forceful but polite message.

EMPLOYEES

Driving and using a mobile phone are both demanding tasks that should not be carried out at the same time.

Responsibility for the safe control of a vehicle always rests with the driver. The law clearly states that you must have proper control of your vehicle.

If it is essential for you to be contacted while you are driving, use voicemail or call diversion and stop regularly to check messages and return calls.

If hands-free equipment is used, it should be installed according to the manufacturers instructions and should follow the British Standards Institution's "Guide to in-vehicle information systems".

(DD 235: 1996)

It can also be an offence for employers to require their employees to use mobile phones while driving.

Do not use a mobile phone close to a vehicle carrying flammable loads.

Ovals:

Driving today requires all of your attention all of the time

Never use a hand-held phone while driving

It is safer not to use a hands-free phone while driving

Use a message service and take regular breaks

Road Safety

DRIVER RESPONSIBILITY

Regardless of how competent a driver claims to be, no-one can hold a phone, obtain a number, conduct a conversation and be in complete control of their vehicle. It is simply not the same as having a conversation with a passenger or listening to a tape or the radio.

It takes less than a split second for a lapse in concentration to result in an accident.

Drivers behaving in this way endanger the safety of the public generally and their own safety too.

THE ADVICE

✔ The only safe way for drivers to use a mobile phone in a vehicle is when they have stopped in a safe place.

✗ Don't distract yourself by using a mobile phone, reading a map or business documents, eating or drinking while driving.

✗ Never use a hand held phone while driving.

✗ Do not fix a mobile phone to the dashboard, in a position where an inflating airbag could dislodge it and push it in your face.

✗ Do not use a mobile phone if there's a danger from petrol spillage or fumes.

Exemplar material

Modelled planning frame

Title page including illustration of computer and/or mobile phone.

Logo of the company producing the leaflet – could be the school logo.

Illustration (clip art?) of a computer in a central place in a home with parent and child working together.

Web site addresses for safety information.

Information about using computers.

Information about using the Internet.

(Exemplar material)

Modelled planning frame (continued)

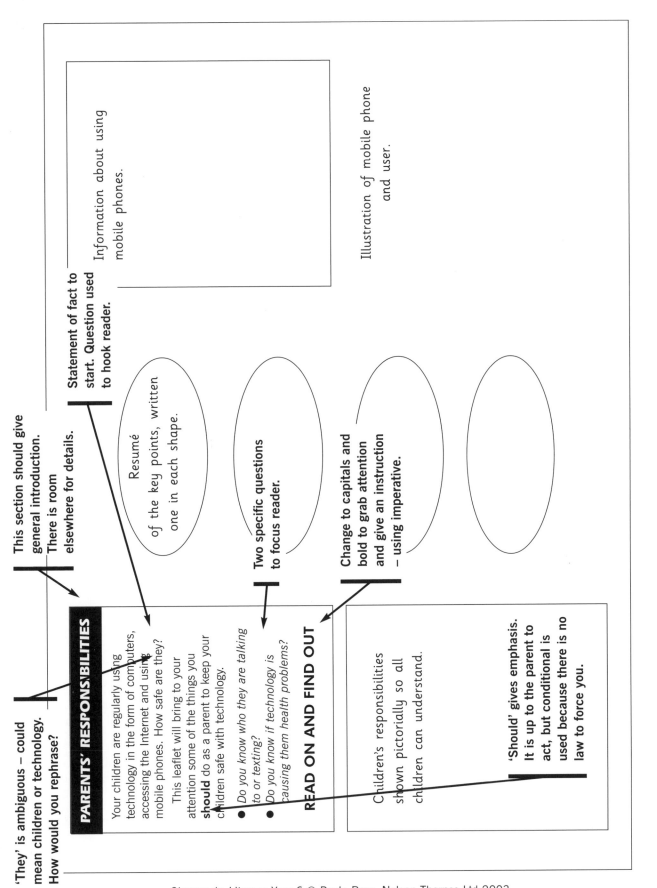

Information about using mobile phones.

Illustration of mobile phone and user.

Statement of fact to start. Question used to hook reader.

This section should give general introduction. There is room elsewhere for details.

Resumé of the key points, written one in each shape.

Two specific questions to focus reader.

Change to capitals and bold to grab attention and give an instruction – using imperative.

'They' is ambiguous – could mean children or technology. How would you rephrase?

PARENTS' RESPONSIBILITIES

Your children are regularly using technology in the form of computers, accessing the Internet and using mobile phones. How safe are they?

This leaflet will bring to your attention some of the things you **should** do as a parent to keep your children safe with technology.

- *Do you know who they are talking to or texting?*
- *Do you know if technology is causing them health problems?*

READ ON AND FIND OUT

Children's responsibilities shown pictorially so all children can understand.

'Should' gives emphasis. It is up to the parent to act, but conditional is used because there is no law to force you.

(**Pupil copymaster**)

Texting

More and more children are using mobile phones for phone calls or text messaging. Here are the issues to be aware of.

▶ HEALTH RISKS The current Government advice, from the Stewart Enquiry in 2000, is that children under 16 should use mobile phones as little as possible because of a possible (but unproven) risk to their brains from the phone's emission of radio waves. In May 2001 the BMA (British Medical Association) produced a report called 'Mobile phones and health' which included this statement: 'Children are particularly likely to use mobile phones for text messaging … Since the handset is normally held near to waist level for this activity, research is necessary into whether mobile phone radiation may affect different parts of the body in different ways, and hence whether there are any additional possible health risks associated with text messaging.'

There are several major research projects around the world looking at mobile phone safety and the BMA expects the final conclusive research findings to be available in two to three years. There are currently conflicting sets of UK research results on the use of hands-free kits (where an earpiece is worn rather than holding the phone to the ear). The *Which? Report* in April 2000 found that using a hands-free kit actually increases the level of emissions entering the skull, whereas Government-commissioned findings in May 2000 contradicted this.

▶ COSTS At 10p per message sent, texting is cheaper than voice calls and using pay-as-you-go vouchers for calls or messages can teach useful budgeting skills.

▶ SECURITY RISKS Parents must teach security rules, for example, never pass on personal information to people you don't know but who contact you through a text message or phone call. Very worryingly, in August 2000 a kids.net survey by NOP found 29 per cent of Web users aged between seven and sixteen would happily supply their postal address to strangers, while 14 per cent would give out their email address.

▶ SAFETY RISKS Just as with email, strangers can make contact via mobile phones, claiming to be someone they are not. Parents should talk to their children about the possible dangers in following up such contacts. Because pay-as-you-go phones are widely available for sale without any registration of the buyer's details, it is impossible to track the ownership of many phones. This has implications for identifying the person responsible for threatening or bullying calls or text messages.

▶ EXPLOITATION RISKS Advertisers recognise the potential of this technology. Already, many big companies are sending advertisements in the form of text messages. In Ibiza last summer, over 3,000 young clubbers registered their mobile numbers so they could receive a variety of messages every day. Children are particularly vulnerable to advertising and this should be an area of concern for parents. Talk to your children about the way advertising works and you can help to make them less vulnerable and more streetwise.

▶ COMMUNICATION PATTERNS Texting currently consists of lots of short, carefully crafted messages, with boys as well as girls keeping in touch with friends and organising their social lives. A recent Vodafone survey of 10 to 21-year-olds found they use text messaging because it is 'Fun, cheap, silent, private and immediate'.

We are already seeing a new genre of text communication with the rise of email – a less formal, more conversational style. Teachers are still developing the literary 'rules' of emailing. Now texting is another genre again and it isn't going to go away.

from **http://www.pin.org.uk/safety/mobilePhones.htm**

(Exemplar material)

Transcribing text into an informal presentation

Select a section and read it through, then go back and underline or highlight the key ideas. Explain this is how to contract information.

Underline this on the board ...	... while you are saying this
HEALTH RISKS The current Government advice, from the Stewart Enquiry in 2000, is that <u>children under 16 should use mobile phones as little as possible</u>	*Highlight key information.*
because of a <u>possible</u> (but unproven) <u>risk to their brains from the phone's emission of radio waves</u>.	*First main point.*
In May 2001 the BMA (British Medical Association) produced a report called 'Mobile phones and health' which included this statement:	*Will this make a difference to the information I am trying to give in the picture? If so include it, if not do not use it as a key point.*
'<u>Children are particularly likely to use mobile phones for text messaging</u> ... Since the <u>handset is normally held near to waist level</u> for this activity, <u>research is necessary</u> into <u>whether mobile phone radiation may affect different parts of the body in different ways</u>,	*Second main point.*
and hence whether there are any additional possible health risks associated with text messaging.'	*Simplify the information so a non-reader or poor reader can understand it.*
There are several major research projects around the world looking at mobile phone safety and the BMA expects the final conclusive research findings to be available in two to three years. There are currently conflicting sets of UK research results on the use of hands-free kits (where an earpiece is worn rather than holding the phone to the ear). The *Which? Report* in April 2000 found that using a hands-free kit actually increases the level of emissions entering the skull, whereas Government-commissioned findings in May 2000 contradicted this.	*This section has no proof at all and actually contradicts and so could be left out.*
	Decide how to present the information as a picture – needs two pictures so one could be a boy and one a girl. Write notes under picture: 'Advice – use mobile phones as little as possible.' Add a subtitle above: 'Up to 16 years'. Go back to the text to ensure you have included all your highlighted key points.

Classworks Literacy Year 6 © Paula Ross, Nelson Thornes Ltd 2003

(Exemplar analysis)

Example of analysis of formal letter about bullying

Address of receiver – known as 'addressee' – on left below sender's address.

Write sender's address (headed paper usually has this at top of page). Include date.

Fairview,
Norman's Cross,
Bywatershire,
NC3 5OA

14th October 2002

Formal start to an unknown recipient.

Secretary for Education,
County Hall,
Bywatershire,
NC1 3AY

Introductory paragraph tells reader subject of letter and gives information about sender.

Dear Sir/Madam,

Formal language (examples underlined).

I enclose copies of correspondence with the headmaster and chairman of governors of Park High School where my daughter Mary continues to be bullied by Jane Brown.

Use of complex sentence and passive voice.

I have asked what measures the school has already taken to halt bullying and what measures it intends to take in the future. The response has been unsatisfactory because the bullying has not stopped, I have not been told what the school is doing and I have not been told of any sanctions against the bullies.

'It' refers to the school, but actually means people in the school – impersonal.

If using word-processing, leave a line between paragraphs rather than indenting.

Please make a formal investigation into my complaint and issue a report. I note from Mary's records that bullying incidents have been recorded. The file reveals action was taken but it has not been successful. I want to know what action the LEA is going to take to ensure the safety of my daughter at this school.

More details of the problem.

Formal connective.

Furthermore, I would like to know how many other complaints of bullying there have been at this school, to staff, the headmaster or the LEA in the past 12 months.

Thank you for your attention to this matter. I look forward to your response at the earliest opportunity.

Yours faithfully

Concluding paragraph – polite but formal tone but indicating some urgency.

A. Gruff

A Gruff (parent)

What the writer wants to happen, with additional details to back up the required action.

Standard English used throughout.

When addressee's name is not known. (When name is known use 'Yours sincerely'.)

A letter to analyse

Canyon View School,
Britsville,
Windsorshire,
BR41 6AS

14th November 2002

Mr Eddie Arnway,
Penguin Books,
375 Hudson Street,
Oxbridge,
OX34 9TY

Dear Mr Arnway,

I am writing on behalf of a group of Year 6 pupils working on a web site design about reading and writing. The group has chosen a few of their favourite authors to interview and would like to publish their answers on the school web site. They would appreciate it if you would respond to their questions and give them permission to publish your answers on their web site.

1. What made you want to write books?
2. What books did you enjoy as a child?
3. What is the hardest part about writing and illustrating books?
4. What did it feel like when you first sold a book?
5. Who is your favourite author and illustrator?
6. Do you follow a schedule or deadline when you write a book?

Thank you for taking your time to answer our questions.

We look forward to hearing from you in the near future and thank you for helping us to complete our project.

Yours sincerely,

Ben Greer

Ben Greer

Classworks Literacy Year 6 © Paula Ross, Nelson Thornes Ltd 2003

(Exemplar material)

Modelled writing of the first paragraph of a formal letter

Write this on the board ...	... while you are saying this
Dear Sir/Madam,	*Unknown recipient – use formal greeting. If word-processed, leave a line between sections and don't indent paragraphs.*
I am writing to you <u>on behalf of</u>	*Formal phrase (examples underlined).*
(insert appropriate name).	*Tells the recipient who is writing.*
(Repeat the name) <u>are</u> very <u>concerned</u>	*Passive voice.*
that children get the most from the tremendous opportunities offered through technology today while at the same time they remain safe.	*Complex sentence stating what the group is about – impersonal.*
(Name of group) have produced a leaflet to help parents to protect their children from any potential hazards.	*Standard English, impersonal and formal tone throughout – explains what the group has done.*
	Correct sign-off.

Classworks Literacy Year 6 © Paula Ross, Nelson Thornes Ltd 2003

Exemplar material

Checklists for formal writing

Example of a checklist for formal writing

- Use an impersonal voice, avoiding personal pronoun 'I'
- Use imperative verbs
- Use passive verbs
- Use formal vocabulary and phrases e.g. 'hereby', 'on behalf of'
- Use technical vocabulary
- Use stilted politeness
- Write in complex sentences
- Possibly include conditionals
- Use standard English to be exact and clear with no ambiguities
- Sound official and weighty – use a formal tone

Example of a checklist for a formal letter

- State who the writer is
- Explain the reason for writing
- Deliver the necessary message/enquiry
- State clearly what the sender would like the recipient to do
- Language can be impersonal
- Use standard English
- Use a formal tone and formal language
- Use formal connectives
- Write sender's name and address top right or centre
- Write recipient's details on left below sender's address
- Leave a line between paragraphs rather than indenting, if word-processed
- Use an appropriate sign-off line

Classworks Literacy Year 6 © Paula Ross, Nelson Thornes Ltd 2003

(Marking ladder)

Marking ladder for a leaflet

Name: _____

Pupil	Objective	Teacher
	My leaflet is split into clearly subtitled sections.	
	I used titles and sub-headings to attract the reader.	
	I used illustrations to support the information.	
	Key information is easily identified through use of colour, shading, boxes, bold and italic, different-shaped sections.	
	I used standard English which is exact and clear with no ambiguities.	
	I used an impersonal tone, avoiding personal pronouns.	
	My vocabulary includes formal phrases and technical words.	
	I used at least three complex sentences.	
	The verbs I used: • include examples of imperative to show compulsion • may include conditionals • may include passive voice.	
	What could I do to improve my formal writing next time?	

(Marking ladder)

Marking ladder for a formal letter

Name: _____

Pupil	Objective	Teacher
	In my formal letter, addresses, date, greeting and sign-off are correctly placed.	
	The first paragraph tells who the writer is and explains the reason for writing.	
	The middle paragraphs deliver the necessary message.	
	The letter states clearly what I would like the recipient to do.	
	I used standard English.	
	I used the appropriate greeting and sign-off.	
	If word-processed, a line space indicates new paragraphs.	
	I used a formal tone (not chatty).	
	What could I do to improve my formal letter writing next time?	

Non-Fiction Texts: Explanation

Outcome

Revision of Science AT4 'Physical Processes – The Earth and Beyond', and aspects of AT3

Objectives

Sentence

1 to revise the language conventions and grammatical features of different types of text such as: narrative, recounts, instructional texts, reports, explanatory texts, persuasive texts, discursive texts.

3 to revise formal styles of writing: the impersonal voice; the use of the passive; management of complex sentences.

Text

15 to secure understanding of the features of explanatory texts from Year 5 term 2.

16 to identify the key features of impersonal formal language, e.g. the present tense, the passive voice and discuss when and why they are used.

Planning frame

- Revise the features of a written explanation, while revising facts about 'The Earth and Beyond'.
- Write an explanation.
- Revise another area of science through the annotation of a science experiment.
- Write up a science experiment linked to 'The Earth and Beyond'.

How you could plan this unit

Day 1	Day 2	Day 3	Day 4	Day 5
Reading and analysis	Reading, modelling and writing	Reading and analysis	Reading, modelling and writing	**Writing for assessment** Plan and write own explanation text based on another scientific area, e.g. the water cycle, using format from Day 2. This could be used to assess the children's understanding of explanation texts and their scientific knowledge of the water cycle
Main Features	*Planning Frames*	*Science Experiments*	*Science Reports*	

Main Features

Objectives

We will understand the purpose of an explanation text, revise the features of explanations and find out how such a text is planned

You need: Resource Pages A–D and K; display paper for checklist.

Whole class work

- Tell the children that this week's work focuses on revising work on writing explanations from Year 5. At the end of the week they will be required to write an explanation on … (insert your chosen scientific theme). In order to do this, you will be reminding them about the features and organisation of explanation writing, looking at the scientific work on 'The Earth and Beyond'.

- *Where are you likely to find explanation writing?* Answer: encyclopedias, manuals for working machines (microwaves, computers), in some parts of non-fiction books (for example, *How did the Romans rule their Empire? How does blood circulate?*), science experiments, DT projects and so on.

- Display Resource Page A. Annotate the main features: clarity of the explanations, use of diagrams and photographs to make the explanation easier to understand, language features (see Resource Page B and checklist 1, Resource Page K).

- As you annotate the text, ask a child to scribe identified features on to the display paper.

- Deconstruct the text to demonstrate how this provides a planning grid for an explanation text (Resource Page C).

- A flow chart is the easiest way to plan an explanation. Flow charts may vary – quickly demonstrate one for an explanation of the water cycle.

Independent, pair or guided work

- Ask the children to read and annotate the information about the Earth (see Resource Page D). Explain that this is the first part of the article and that tomorrow they will write part of the explanation which is missing.

- Remind the children to refer to the checklist.

Plenary

- Review the features of explanation writing identified in Resource Page D.

- Ask the children to work in pairs to deconstruct the text into a planning frame. Each pair should then explain their planning grid to another pair.

161

Planning Frames

Objective

We will use a planning grid and write an explanation for the occurrence of day and night

You need: Resource Pages D–F and K; science books on the Earth in space.

Whole class work

- Remind the children that they need to finish analysing and annotating the text from the previous lesson (Resource Page D).

- Look at the 'Earth and Beyond' section of a science book. *What additional information about the Earth do you need to add to the planning frame?*

> The Earth rotates on its axis causing day and night.
>
> The Earth takes a year to orbit the Sun.
>
> The height of the Sun in the sky varies with the seasons.
>
> The length of shadows depends on the position of the Sun.

- Draw one of the children's planning frames on the board and model adding other sections to include the missing information (Resource Page E).

- Review the checklist (Resource Page K) and model writing the paragraph about the Earth orbiting the Sun (Resource Page F). Keep referring to the features the children identified in the previous lesson.

- Refer the children to the information in the science textbook about the Earth rotating on its axis causing day and night to occur.

Independent, pair or guided work

- The children write and draw diagrams to explain how the movement of the Earth in space causes night and day.

- Encourage them to include details about why the spinning of the Earth on its axis causes the Sun to *appear* to move across the sky. *What is actually happening?*

- Some children might go on to write a further paragraph to add to your modelled example to explain how the height of the Sun in the sky varies with time of year.

Plenary

- The children's response partners read the explanatory paragraphs. They should check for clarity of information and other features from the checklist.

- Select one or two that worked well for appraisal by the class. Elicit responses to outline why the explanation worked well.

Science Experiments

Objective

We will analyse and annotate explanation texts, referring to the class checklist of features

You need: Resource Pages G–I and K.

Whole class work

- Review where explanation texts are likely to be found (see 'Main features' lesson plan page). Explain that this lesson will focus on a write-up of a science experiment – another kind of explanation text.

- Display Resource Page G. Analyse and annotate the main features of the genre (see Resource Page H), linking these to features found in the original explanation text: passive voice, present tense for the conclusion, causal language and technical language. Emphasise the importance of clear layout.

- As features are annotated, ask a child to add them to the class checklist (see Resource Page K for ideas).

- Remind the children of when and how they covered this work in their science lessons and what they need to know for the SATs.

Independent, pair or guided work

- Ask the children to analyse and annotate the experiment to investigate the effect of burning on different materials (Resource Page I).

Plenary

- In pairs, the children refer to the class checklist to see if all the features from your analysis and annotation have been noted.

- Call out a few phrases or sentences and ask if they would be seen in explanation writing. For example:

> The wood was held above the flame for 10 seconds. (Yes.)
>
> I saw the flame burning the paper. (No.)
>
> We used a candle and some tongs. (No.)
>
> The flame burned the paper. (Yes.)

Science Reports

Objective

We will write an explanation in the form of a science report, using the features from the checklist

You need: Resource Pages E and J–L.

Whole class work

- Display your planning frame (Resource Page E). Point out that the section on length of shadows produced by the Sun has not yet been written. *The focus of today's lesson is to produce a science experiment write-up (report) to go with the explanation of the Earth and Beyond.*

- Question the children about the experiment they carried out in Year 5 into the length of shadows (QCA Unit 5E 'Earth, Sun and Moon' objective – the Sun appears to move across the sky over the course of a day). Review the scientific facts. Make notes on the board about the experiment.

- Use the notes to model the experiment. Start by modelling a title that explains what the experiment is about:

> An experiment to investigate if shadows stay the same length throughout the day.

- Remind the children of the format of a science write-up and briefly revise the apparatus and diagram sections. Explain that you are going to model the method part, and that the children will be adding the rest of the information in independent time. Model writing, using Resource Page J.

- Review the experiment report so far. *What else is needed?* Refer to the checklist (Resource Page K) for ideas.

Independent, pair or guided work

- The children complete the report by adding the apparatus and diagram sections, the results and conclusion.

- Ask the children to imagine that the reader had not carried out the practical experiment. Children read through their response partner's work and consider whether it has been written so that someone else can clearly understand what has been explained.

- You may wish to refer to the unit in *Classworks* Literacy Year 5 on Instruction Writing, page 1.

Plenary

- Ask the children to use the marking ladder (Resource Page L) to assess their explanations for 'How the movement of the Earth in space causes night and day', and the experiment to investigate if length of shadows stays the same throughout the day.

(Exemplar material)

The Moon

A moon is a large body or mass of material that orbits around a planet. It is usually much smaller than the planet. The diameter of the Earth's Moon is 2 160 miles. This compares with the diameter of the Earth at about 4 000 miles. The Earth has only one moon. Mars has two moons, while Jupiter has nine moons.

The Moon orbits around the Earth, taking approximately 29½ days for a complete orbit. The Moon rotates on its axis at the same rate, such that the same side of the Moon always faces the Earth.

As the Moon travels around the Earth, different views of the side that is illuminated by the Sun and the side that is dark are seen. The views create the different phases of the Moon. Consequently at different times of the month, the Moon can appear like a crescent, half circle, or full. The Moon is sometimes visible in the daytime. The Moon appears brighter at night because of sunlight that is reflected off its surface.

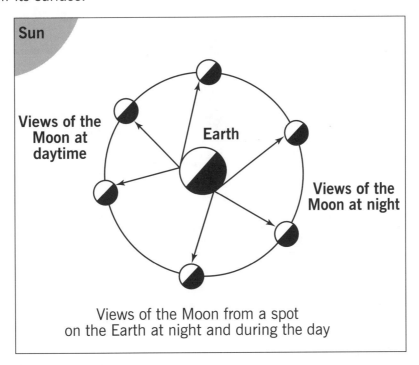

Views of the Moon from a spot
on the Earth at night and during the day

Furthermore, the gravity of the Moon is one-sixth the gravity on the Earth. This means that a person who has a mass of 90 kg on Earth would have a mass of only 15 kg, if measured on the Moon. That is why the astronauts were able to jump so high when they were on the Moon. The force of gravity from the Moon affects the Earth. Its gravity reaches the Earth and pulls the oceans toward the Moon, causing the tides.

see **http://www.schoolforchampions.com/science/moon.htm**

(Exemplar analysis)

Example of analysis of *The Moon*

Present tense.

Technical vocabulary.

Introduction to orientate the reader by giving general information.

Specific details.

Causal language.

A moon is a large body or mass of material that orbits around a planet. It is usually much smaller than the planet. The diameter of the Earth's Moon is 2 160 miles. This compares with the diameter of the Earth at about 4 000 miles. The Earth has only one moon. Mars has two moons, while Jupiter has nine moons.

Written in the third person throughout.

The Moon orbits around the Earth, taking approximately 29½ days for a complete orbit. The Moon rotates on its axis at the same rate, such that the same side of the Moon always faces the Earth.

Passive voice.

As the Moon travels around the Earth, different views of the side that is illuminated by the Sun and the side that is dark are seen. The views create the different phases of the Moon. Consequently at different times of the month, the Moon can appear like a crescent, half circle, or full. The Moon is sometimes visible in the daytime. The Moon appears brighter at night because of sunlight that is reflected off its surface.

Formal vocabulary used instead of 'look'.

Formal vocabulary used instead of 'can be seen'.

Formal connective.

Impersonal language throughout – no personal pronouns.

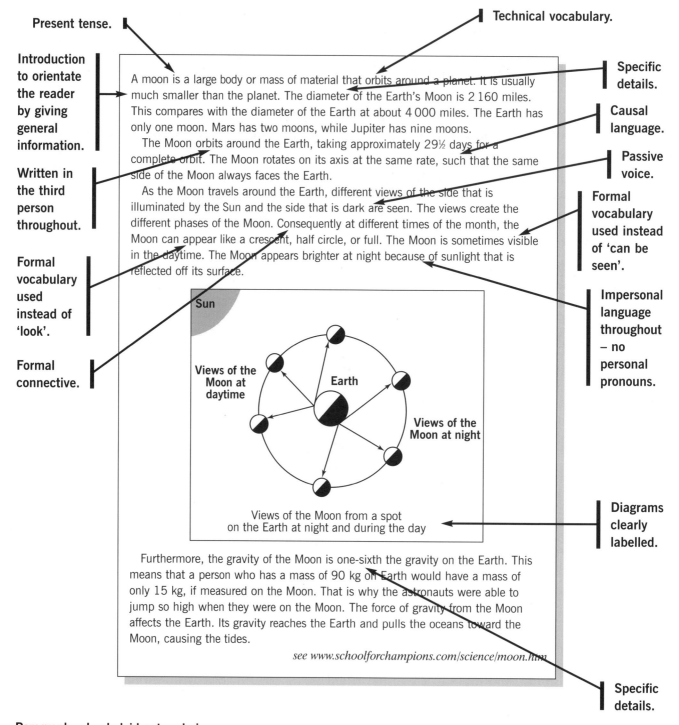

Sun

Views of the Moon at daytime

Earth

Views of the Moon at night

Views of the Moon from a spot
on the Earth at night and during the day

Diagrams clearly labelled.

Furthermore, the gravity of the Moon is one-sixth the gravity on the Earth. This means that a person who has a mass of 90 kg on Earth would have a mass of only 15 kg, if measured on the Moon. That is why the astronauts were able to jump so high when they were on the Moon. The force of gravity from the Moon affects the Earth. Its gravity reaches the Earth and pulls the oceans toward the Moon, causing the tides.

see www.schoolforchampions.com/science/moon.htm

Specific details.

Paragraphs clearly laid out and give order to the explanation: 1 = intro, 2 = orbiting, 3 = phases, 4 = gravity.

(Exemplar material)

Deconstructing the text – commentary

- Explanations usually have a series of logical steps.

- The Moon explanation gives a general introduction.

- It then takes an important idea – motion of the Moon ... [*Add 1st arrow between the two planning circles*]

- ... which causes the phases so it is logical to link these two paragraphs. [*Add 2nd arrow*]

- Then another important idea – gravity ... [*Add 3rd arrow*]

- ... which causes tides on Earth.

- The order of the paragraphs needs careful consideration. Try to make the order a series of logical steps wherever possible.

- A final paragraph will round off the explanation by adding some general remarks.

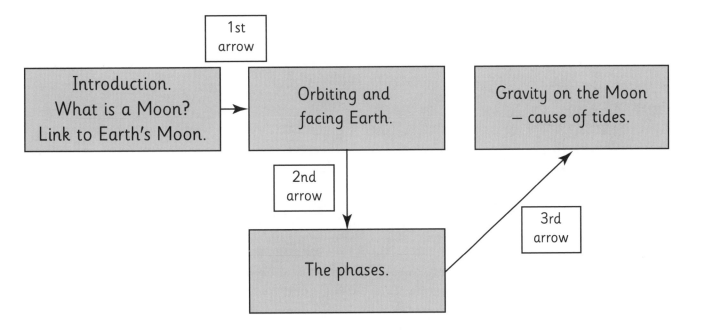

(**Pupil copymaster**)

The Earth

The Earth is a rotating sphere that orbits the Sun. Its tilt causes it to have seasons of warmer and colder weather. Its unique relationship with the Sun allows it to sustain life. The Earth also has a magnetic field.

The Earth is approximately a sphere. The shape of the Earth is similar to that of the Moon and the Sun: spherical like a ball or a globe. This has been proven by space vehicles circling the Earth, as well as from photographs of the Earth taken from space. Its globe shape is slightly flattened at the poles.

As well as orbiting the sun, the axis of the Earth tilts. The tilt is always in the same direction.

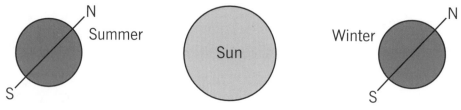

The tilt of the Earth is in the same direction

The reason the seasons change has to do with how directly the Sun is shining on that particular part of the Earth. When the Northern half of the Earth (or Northern Hemisphere) is in the part of the orbit around the Sun where the sunlight shines more directly on it, the days are longer and less sunlight is reflected. That is summer, and the weather becomes warmer.

Sunlight shines more directly in summer

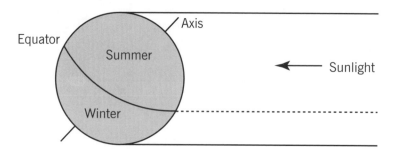

Due to the spherical shape of the Earth, there is more daylight in the summer the closer you get to the pole. When you cross the Arctic Circle in the Northern Hemisphere or the Antarctic Circle in the Southern Hemisphere, daylight can last for 24 hours in summer. That is why it is called 'the land of the midnight Sun'.

On the other side of the orbit around the Sun, the angle of the sunlight is steeper, resulting in more light being reflected. Also, the days are shorter. This results in the colder weather of winter.

Sunlight reflects off at a steeper angle in winter

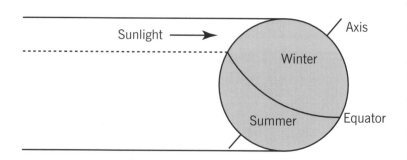

Classworks Literacy Year 6 © Paula Ross, Nelson Thornes Ltd 2003

(Exemplar material)

Modelled planning frame

This example may need to be amended in the light of the planning produced by the class in the plenary, Day 1.

- *What properties of the Earth are causing other things to happen?*
- *The effect of the Earth on these things needs to be linked into the main facts about the Earth.*

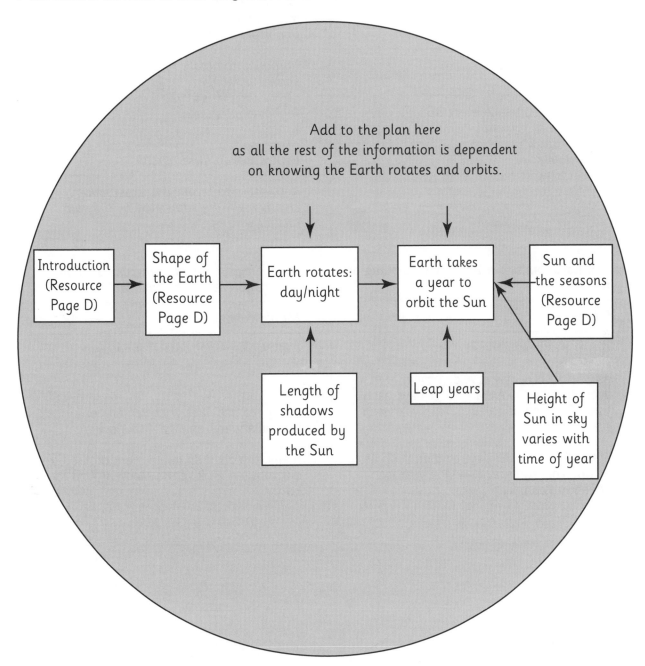

As you build this grid remind the children:

- *Shadow length is caused by the Earth rotating.*
- *Leap years are caused by the length of time the Earth takes to orbit the Sun.*
- *Seasons are caused by the tilt of the Earth as it orbits the Sun.*

(Exemplar material)

Modelled writing

Write this on the board ...	... while you are saying this
	Work logically – start with the most important fact and then add other information which is reliant on the important fact.
The Earth revolves	*Introduce the main fact. Present tense. Formal language.*
around the Sun once every 365.25 days. The shape of the orbit	*Technical language.*
is an ellipse.	*Impersonal in third person.*
The Earth orbits the Sun while spinning on its axis.	*Remember to layout the explanation clearly – writing supported by diagram, further writing.* *Label diagrams to help the explanation. Information reliant on first fact.*
Since	*Formal connective.*
a year has been defined	*Passive voice and formal language.*
as 365 days, a day is added every four years to total the extra quarter days each year. That year is called a 'leap year' and ~~comes~~	[Write 'comes' first, then remember formal vocabulary and change it to 'occurs'.]
occurs on years divisible by four, such as 2004. The extra day in a leap year is added in February.	[Later, the children could mark on the diagram the orbit of the Moon around the Earth.]

(Pupil copymaster)

Write-up of a science experiment

Experiment to investigate if stirring affects the rate of dissolving

Apparatus

2 pots, measuring pot, water, salt, and teaspoon.

Diagram

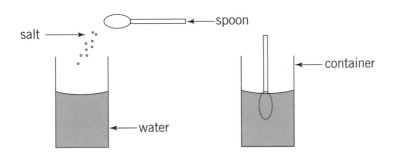

Method

The factors that were kept the same: temperature, amount of water, amount of salt, size of pot, size of salt particles.

The factor that was changed: one pot was stirred.

What was measured or observed: the salt in the water.

100ml of water was measured and poured into a container. This was repeated in an identical container. Two teaspoons of salt were added to each container. The salt in one container was stirred.

Results

The salt in the container that was stirred dissolved. The salt in the container that was not stirred did not dissolve.

Conclusion

The experiment shows that stirring helps salt dissolve faster in water. The more stirring, the faster the salt will dissolve. This is because the stirring action helps break up the molecules so they spread out among the molecules of the liquid.

(Exemplar analysis)

Example of analysis of write-up of a science experiment

Point out difference between a diagram (all items in a simplified form) and a picture (3D with accurate representation of all items).

Title – recognised format 'Experiment to investigate ...' with clear description of what is to be investigated.

List separated by commas.

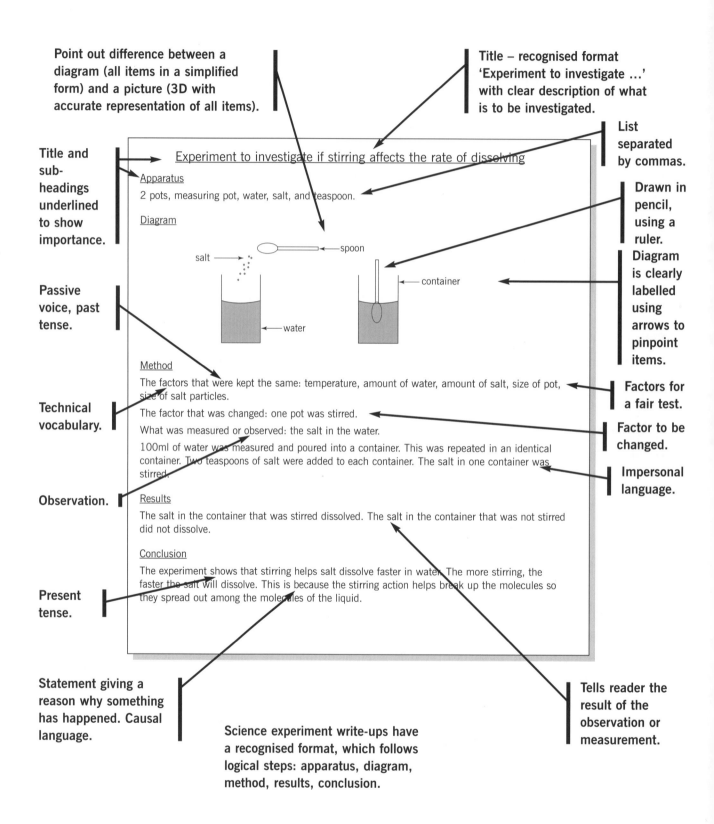

Title and sub-headings underlined to show importance.

Experiment to investigate if stirring affects the rate of dissolving

Apparatus

2 pots, measuring pot, water, salt, and teaspoon.

Diagram

salt → ・ spoon

spoon

← container

water

Method

The factors that were kept the same: temperature, amount of water, amount of salt, size of pot, size of salt particles.

The factor that was changed: one pot was stirred.

What was measured or observed: the salt in the water.

100ml of water was measured and poured into a container. This was repeated in an identical container. Two teaspoons of salt were added to each container. The salt in one container was stirred.

Results

The salt in the container that was stirred dissolved. The salt in the container that was not stirred did not dissolve.

Conclusion

The experiment shows that stirring helps salt dissolve faster in water. The more stirring, the faster the salt will dissolve. This is because the stirring action helps break up the molecules so they spread out among the molecules of the liquid.

Passive voice, past tense.

Technical vocabulary.

Observation.

Present tense.

Drawn in pencil, using a ruler.

Diagram is clearly labelled using arrows to pinpoint items.

Factors for a fair test.

Factor to be changed.

Impersonal language.

Statement giving a reason why something has happened. Causal language.

Science experiment write-ups have a recognised format, which follows logical steps: apparatus, diagram, method, results, conclusion.

Tells reader the result of the observation or measurement.

Classworks Literacy Year 6 © Paula Ross, Nelson Thornes Ltd 2003

(Pupil copymaster)

Another science experiment

Experiment to investigate the effect of burning on different materials

<u>Apparatus</u>

Candle (nightlight), metal tray of dry sand, tongs, matches, fire blanket for safety.

Materials: 5cm x 5cm piece of cotton fabric

                  5cm x 5cm piece of paper

                  piece of cheese

                  a twig

<u>Diagram</u>

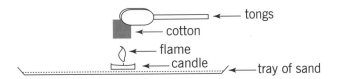

<u>Method</u>

The factors that were kept the same: candle, amount of time in the flame, distance of material from the flame.

The factor that was changed: different materials were placed in the flame.

What was measured or observed: how materials changed and any new materials that were made.

The candle was placed in the centre of the tray of sand and the wick was lit. In turn different materials were held by tongs and placed at the same point in the candle flame for 15 seconds. Observations were made of what happened to each material.

<u>Results</u>

The twig blackened and smoked. The paper smoked and quickly caught alight, producing another flame and then left a residue of dark ash. The cheese melted and dripped into the tray. The fabric turned black, smoke appeared and then it burned leaving a residue of ash.

<u>Conclusion</u>

The experiment showed that when materials are burnt, there are different reactions. Some burn and others melt. These are irreversible reactions because new materials are made.

(Exemplar material)

Shadows experiment

Write this on the board ...	... while you are saying this
The factors	*Technical vocabulary.*
that were kept the same:	Ask: *What should I add here?*
The factor that was changed:	Ask: *What should I add here?*
What was measured or observed:	Ask: *What should I add here?*
The experiment was carried out	*Passive voice, past tense.*
on a sunny, cloudless day. We stood a metre stick on the playground.	[Rehearse the sentence aloud and then change to the correct format.] *That doesn't sound right – it should be in the passive voice.*
A metre-long	*Precise vocabulary.*
stick was placed	*Passive voice, past tense.*
upright on the playground. At hourly intervals throughout the day, the shadow of the stick was observed and drawn	*Passive voice, past tense.*
in chalk on to the playground. The time was ~~written~~	[Change your mind and cross out.]
recorded	*More formal language.*
next to the shadow. The length of the shadow was measured and recorded.	*Passive voice, past tense.*

(Exemplar material)

Checklists for non-fiction texts: explanation

Example of a checklist for an explanation text ①

- Explain in a series of logical steps

- Use present tense (except historical explanations)

- Use causal language, e.g. 'because', 'the reason that', 'this results in', and so on

- Use impersonal language

- Use technical vocabulary

- Lay out the text clearly

- Label diagrams clearly

- Include boxes for extra information

- Write in the third person

- Use the passive voice

- Usually use formal vocabulary, e.g. 'placed' instead of 'put'

- Use formal connectives – 'furthermore', 'therefore', 'consequently'

Example of a checklist for a science experiment write-up ②

- Choose a title such as: 'Experiment to investigate/show ...' (clear indication of the investigation)

- Lay out the text clearly, using recognised subtitles
  - apparatus (equipment used)
  - diagram (how equipment was set up)
  - method (how experiment was carried out)
  - results (what happened)
  - conclusion (what was discovered and why it happened)

- Draw diagrams in pencil with clear labels

- Under the method, include:
  - the factors that stay the same
  - the factor to be changed
  - what is to be measured or observed

- Write in the passive voice

- Use past tense for what happened (method and results)

- Use present tense for the conclusion

- Use causal language in the conclusion – explaining scientifically why it happened

- Use technical language

Marking ladder

Name: _____

Pupil	Objective	Teacher
	The title sets up the explanation.	
	My layout is clear and uses paragraphs or subtitles.	
	Any illustrations add to the explanation and are clearly labelled.	
	My vocabulary includes: • technical language • precise details • formal language, e.g. 'recorded' instead of 'written'.	
	My explanation gives an impersonal view.	
	I used the passive voice, and mainly the present tense.	
	I used causal connectives, e.g. 'because', 'this results in'.	
	My explanation is easy to understand because it is written in a series of logical steps.	
	What could I do to improve my explanation writing next time?	

Poetry on a Theme: 'The Sea'

Outcome

A class anthology on the theme of 'The Sea'

Objectives

Sentence

2 to conduct detailed language investigations through interviews, research and reading, e.g. of proverbs, language change over time, dialect, study of headlines.

Text

2 to discuss how linked poems relate to one another by themes, format and repetition, e.g. cycle of poems about the seasons.

3 to describe and evaluate the style of an individual poet.

4 to comment critically on the overall impact of a poem, showing how language and themes have been developed.

7 to annotate passages in detail in response to specific questions.

12 to compare texts in writing, drawing out:
   - their different styles and preoccupations;
   - their strengths and weaknesses;
   - their different values and appeal to a reader.

13 to write a sequence of poems linked by theme or form, e.g. a haiku calendar.

Planning frame

- Read a selection of poems on the theme of the sea and annotate typical features.

- Compare the texts in writing.

- Read and annotate two poems by Charles Causley.

- Use the structure to write extra stanzas or own poem.

- Investigate the use of unusual language and invent words to use in own poems.

Notes

- This unit could link with QCA Geography Unit 23 'Investigating Coasts' or be adapted to link with QCA Geography Unit 14 'Investigating Rivers'.

- You may wish to make available other poems to provide extra stimulus for writing. For example, *The Wreck of the Hesperus*, by Henry Wadsworth Longfellow; *A Sea-Spell*, by Dante Gabriel Rossetti; *The Sea*, by Lewis Carroll; *By the Sea*, by William Wordsworth; *Annabel Lee*, by Edgar Alan Poe; *Sweet and Low, by* Alfred, Lord Tennyson.

How you could plan this unit

Day 1	Day 2	Day 3	Day 4	Day 5
Reading and analysis	**Modelling and writing**	**Modelling and writing**	**Reading and analysis** Ask specific questions about the poems. Annotate relevant stanzas to show where to locate answers and read for implicit information	**Modelling and writing** Select a poet and evaluate his or her style and overall impact of selected poem(s)
Unpicking the Meaning	*Comparing Poems*	*A Written Comparison*		

Day 6	Day 7	Day 8	Day 9	Day 10
Reading and analysis Read and annotate poems with unusual language structure	**Modelling and writing** Write a poem with invented words	**Reading and analysis, modelling and writing**	**Reading and analysis** Use *What sailors say*, by Charles Causley, to study proverbs	**Performance** Complete anthology and perform some of the poems
		Charles Causley		

Unpicking the Meaning

Objectives

We will discuss how poems with the same theme relate to one another. We will develop strategies for unpicking the meaning of a poem, and revise the language and text features for poetry

You need: Resource Pages A–D, J, L and M; other poems about the sea; display paper; dictionaries.

Whole class work

- Explain that in this unit the children will compare poems on the theme of 'The Sea', and look critically at particular poets' work and unpick the meaning of poems. They will use this knowledge to compose their own poems for a class anthology.

- *In order to unpick a poem when its meaning is not so clear you will need to refer to your knowledge of different types of poems and the language features that poets use, and then use clues in the poem to help you unpick the rest.*

- In pairs, give the children three minutes to list as many different types of poem as they can. Ask for a brief definition of each. Write each type on a leaf shape, with the definition written on the reverse, and hang from a cut branch to make a 'poet-tree' for class display.

  > narrative poems, blank verse, cinquains, shape poems, tanka, list poems, kennings, haiku, sonnets …

- Share a selection of poems written on the theme of 'The Sea' (see Resource Pages A, B, J and L; see also the earlier unit on Long-established Poets, p11). Ask the children to identify any particular types of poetry from the examples, for example: *My Granny* = quatrain.

- Demonstrate how to analyse and annotate *A Wanderer's Song* (Resource Page C).

- *From the first read-through, try to get an idea of what the poem is about*. Read aloud to the class including the title. *From the title I know it is about a person who spends his life wandering around. From the stanzas (verses), I think he wants to stop wandering the land and go off to sea.*

- *In the second reading you need evidence to back up your intuitions. You can unpick the poem further by looking at word choice and language features chosen.*

- Start to formulate two checklists: one identifying strategies for unpicking a poem's meaning, the other language features used by poets (see Resource Page M for ideas).

- Return to the poem and add a label to each stanza to sum it up (Resource Page D).

Independent, pair or guided work

- Ask the children to select a poem they enjoyed but found difficult to understand. They try to unpick the meaning ('deconstruct').

- Encourage the children to refer to displayed checklists.

Plenary

- The children work in groups on their chosen poem. Allow time to discuss what they found out. One person gives a brief summary to the rest of the class.

- Ask the children what language features they noticed and add to the class checklist.

Comparing Poems

Objectives

We will identify the similarities and differences in poems on the same theme and produce a plan to compare them. We will also identify why a poem might appeal to a reader

You need: Resource Pages E–G; a selection of poems on the same theme.

Whole class work

- Explain that the focus of the next two lessons is on learning how to write a comparison of poems.

- Remind the children of the poems shared in the previous lesson. Select *Disevolving* and *Sea Fever* (Resource Page E) to compare.

- *To compare the poems, you need to identify which elements are similar and which are different.*

- Display the planning frame (Resource Page F) and explain the subtitles you have selected to help find the appropriate information. As the similarities and differences are found, model writing these into a planning frame (see Resource Page G).

- Point out that some of the identified areas will be facts: for example, blank verse, rhyming couplets; other areas such as strengths, weaknesses and appeal are *opinions* not *facts*.

Independent, pair or guided work

- The children choose two poems on similar themes and complete a planning frame for comparison. Some children might prefer to select one of the modelled poems and one of their own choice.

- Remind the children of the previous day's work on how to unpick a poem for meaning, which will help when looking for similarities and differences.

Plenary

- Select a child's planning frame to read aloud to the class. Identify the poems only as A and B. At the end of the plan ask the children to identify which two poems were being compared. *How did you know?*

- *Did anybody disagree with any of the arguments put forward?* Re-emphasise that different opinions are allowable, provided they are backed up with evidence.

- Repeat with two different poems.

A Written Comparison

Objective

We will use connectives of comparison and contrast and produce a written comparison of the poems from planning frame notes

You need: Resource Pages F, G and M; whiteboards or notepaper.

Whole class work

- Explain that the focus of the lesson is to learn how to write a comparison of poems from the planning frames completed in the previous lesson. Display and read aloud the modelled grid (Resource Page G).

- Explain that the comparison can be split into three parts: an introduction, the main body and the conclusion.

- Decide whether to model the whole comparison in one session or to model each section and give the children time to write their own version before modelling the next section.

- Take the opportunity to revise the use of connectives for comparison and contrast (Resource Page F). Ask a child to add features to a class checklist as you demonstrate the process of writing a comparison (see Resource Page M for ideas).

Independent, pair or guided work

- The children write a comparison of their chosen poems, using the notes in their planning frames. Encourage them to use the class checklists of features.

Plenary

- On whiteboards or paper, the children make a simple chart like the planning frame:

	Poem A	Poem B
Type		
Subject		
Strengths		
Weaknesses		
Mood		
Appeal		

- As the comparison is read aloud, ask the children to tick the relevant section of their chart as they hear each category mentioned in the comparison.

Charles Causley

Objectives

We will show how language and themes have been developed in Charles Causley's poems. We will then write another verse for one of Causley's poems or a poem with a similar theme

You need: Resource Pages J–L; thesauruses.

Whole class work

- *This lesson looks at two poems about the sea written in a similar style by Charles Causley.* Explain that the children will learn to deconstruct the verses in order to see how Causley develops his poems through his choice of language and structure.

- The children will use the deconstruction to help them add an additional stanza to the poems or write their own version using the identified structure.

- Display and read *Morwenstow* and *How the Sea* (Resource Pages J and L). Ask for first reactions to the poems. **How are they similar?** Answer: both show the sea talking (personification) and someone asking questions.

- Demonstrate how to deconstruct *Morwenstow* (Resource Page K), highlighting patterns, choice of language, length of lines and how extra details are written into the questions.

- In pairs, the children think of another question to ask the sea, for example:

  > Why are you rough, sea?

  Select one suggestion and model looking up the keyword in the question ('rough') in a thesaurus to find a similar word to use in the follow-up question.

- The children use this word to think of a second question. Encourage them to read aloud their questions to see if they fit the pattern of the poem.

- *How would the sea answer?*

Independent, pair or guided work

- In pairs or small groups, the children analyse and annotate *How the Sea* (Resource Page I).

- Encourage the children to use a thesaurus to find other words similar to 'shout', 'cries' and 'moans' and then other options for 'wreck', 'freight', 'sailor'.

- Work collaboratively to invent a new stanza for the poem or the children's own poems using a similar structure.

Plenary

- Ask the children to read their new stanzas. The rest of the class should decide if they followed the structure of the original poem. Use a response sandwich to evaluate: one positive comment; one idea for improvement; another positive comment.

Pupil copymaster

My Granny

My Granny is an octopus
At the bottom of the sea,
And when she comes to supper
She brings her family.

She chooses a wild wet night
When the world rolls blind
As a boulder in the night-sea surf,
And her family troops behind.

The sea-smell enters with them
As they sidle and slither and spill
With their huge eyes and their tiny eyes
And a dripping ocean-chill.

Some of her cousins are lobsters
Some floppy jellyfish —
What would you be if your family tree
Grew out of such a dish?

Her brothers are crabs jointed and knobbed
With little pinhead eyes,
Their pincers crack the biscuits
And they bubble joyful cries.

Crayfish the size of ponies
Creak as they sip their milk.
My father stares in horror
At my mother's secret ilk.

They wave long whiplash antennae,
They sizzle and they squirt —
We smile and waggle our fingers back
Or Grandma would be hurt.

"What's new, Ma?" my father asks,
"Down in the marvelous deep?"
Her face swells up, her eyes bulge huge
And she begins to weep.

She knots her sucker tentacles
And gapes like a nestling bird,
And her eyes flash, changing stations,
As she attempts a WORD —

Then out of her eyes there brim two drops
That plop into her saucer —
And that is all she manages,
And my Dad knows he can't force her.

And when they've gone, my ocean folk
No man could prove they came —
For the sea tears in her saucer
And a man's tears are the same.

Ted Hughes, in Unzip Your Lips,
poems chosen by Paul Cookson

A Wanderer's Song

A wind's in the heart of me, a fire's in my heels,
I am tired of brick and stone and rumbling wagon-wheels;

I hunger for the sea's edge, the limit of the land,
Where the wild old Atlantic is shouting on the sand.

Oh I'll be going, leaving the noises of the street,
To where a lifting foresail-foot is yanking at the sheet;

To a windy, tossing anchorage where yawls and ketches ride,
Oh I'll be going, going, until I meet the tide.

And first I'll hear the sea-wind, the mewing of the gulls,
The clucking, sucking of the sea about the rusty hulls,

The songs at the capstan at the hooker warping out,
And then the heart of me'll know I'm there or thereabout.

Oh I am sick of brick and stone, the heart of me is sick,
For windy green, unquiet sea, the realm of Moby Dick;

And I'll be going, going, from the roaring of the wheels,
For a wind's in the heart of me, a fire's in my heels.

John Masefield, from Salt Water Ballads *(1902)*

(Exemplar analysis)

Example of analysis of *A Wanderer's Song*

Personification used to give an image – things that are strong and fast-moving are pushing him into changing his life.

Sensible guess: he is a stonemason. Identify format: rhyming couplets. Reading to rhythm helps meaning.

Repeats 'sea's edge' in different words ('limit of land') to reinforce how desperate he is.

Reference to ocean by name.

Personification builds on image of 'wild' Atlantic.

Where mainsail is attached. (Sheet = sail.)

Phrase repeated several times during poem – important.

Personification.

Apparatus for lifting weights by winding in a cable.

Masted ships.

Sounds he will hear to tell him he is nearing coast. (He will also hear songs of men at work moving old boat.)

Goes back to start of poem and repeats how fed up he is with present life and his wish to go to sea.

Being moved by hauling on a line fastened to an anchor – in this case, the capstan.

Repeats first sentence to conclude poem.

Worn-out boat.

A wind's in the heart of me, a fire's in my heels,
I am tired of brick and stone and rumbling wagon-wheels;

I hunger for the sea's edge, the limit of the land,
Where the wild old Atlantic is shouting on the sand.

Oh I'll be going, leaving the noises of the street,
To where a lifting foresail-foot is yanking at the sheet;

To a windy, tossing anchorage where yawls and ketches ride,
Oh I'll be going, going, until I meet the tide.

And first I'll hear the sea-wind, the mewing of the gulls,
The clucking, sucking of the sea about the rusty hulls,

The songs at the capstan at the hooker warping out,
And then the heart of me'll know I'm there or thereabout.

Oh I am sick of brick and stone, the heart of me is sick,
For windy green, unquiet sea, the realm of Moby Dick;

And I'll be going, going, from the roaring of the wheels,
For a wind's in the heart of me, a fire's in my heels.

John Masefield, from Salt Water Ballads *(1902)*

Classworks Literacy Year 6 © Paula Ross, Nelson Thornes Ltd 2003

(Exemplar analysis)

Example of labelling stanzas of *A Wanderer's Song*

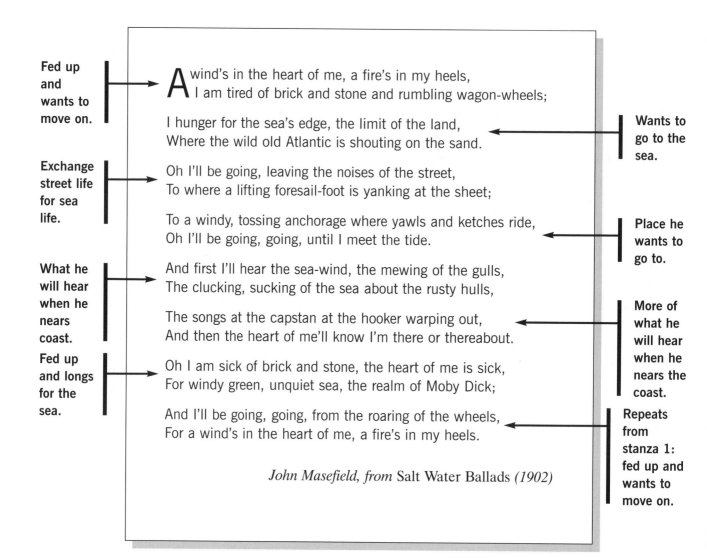

Fed up and wants to move on.

A wind's in the heart of me, a fire's in my heels,
I am tired of brick and stone and rumbling wagon-wheels;

I hunger for the sea's edge, the limit of the land,
Where the wild old Atlantic is shouting on the sand.

Wants to go to the sea.

Exchange street life for sea life.

Oh I'll be going, leaving the noises of the street,
To where a lifting foresail-foot is yanking at the sheet;

To a windy, tossing anchorage where yawls and ketches ride,
Oh I'll be going, going, until I meet the tide.

Place he wants to go to.

What he will hear when he nears coast.

And first I'll hear the sea-wind, the mewing of the gulls,
The clucking, sucking of the sea about the rusty hulls,

The songs at the capstan at the hooker warping out,
And then the heart of me'll know I'm there or thereabout.

More of what he will hear when he nears the coast.

Fed up and longs for the sea.

Oh I am sick of brick and stone, the heart of me is sick,
For windy green, unquiet sea, the realm of Moby Dick;

And I'll be going, going, from the roaring of the wheels,
For a wind's in the heart of me, a fire's in my heels.

Repeats from stanza 1: fed up and wants to move on.

John Masefield, from Salt Water Ballads *(1902)*

Two Poems to Compare

Sea Fever

I must go down to the sea again, to the lonely sea and the sky,
And all I ask is a tall ship and a star to steer her by,
And the wheel's kick and the wind's song and the white sail's shaking,
And a grey mist on the sea's face and a grey dawn breaking.

I must go down to the seas again, for the call of the running tide
Is a wild call and a clear call that may not be denied;
And all I ask is a windy day with the white clouds flying,
And the flung spray and the blown spume, and the sea-gulls crying.

I must go down to the seas again, to the vagrant gypsy life,
To the gull's way and the whale's way, where the wind's like a whetted knife;
And all I ask is a merry yarn from a laughing fellow-rover,
And quiet sleep and a sweet dream when the long trick's over.

John Masefield, from Salt Water Ballads *(1902)*

Disevolving

As a child it was fun
To spring from the towels, aiming straight at the sea,
And have it wrestle me,
My quick stride quenched to slow-motion,
Until – at waist-high –
I could make better going
By lifting up horizontal
And flapping my limbs
Fish-wise.

Joseph Johnson, from Words on Water

(Pupil copymaster)

Planning frame

	Poem 1	Poem 2
Type of poem		
Subject of the poem		
Strengths		
Weaknesses		
Mood		
Appeal to the reader		

(Exemplar material)

Modelled comparison of poems

	Sea Fever, by John Masefield	*Disevolving*, by Joseph Johnson
Type of poem	● Rhyming poem ● Quatrain set out in rhyming couplets	● Blank verse ● One rhyme: 'me' and 'sea'
Subject of the poem	● Someone who wants to go to the sea again ● Memories of what will be found at the sea ● What the narrator wants to experience again	● A child trying to move in the sea ● Narrator remembering what it was like
Strengths	● Strong rhythm, helped by repeated phrases ● A theme which appeals to many people	● Good description of what actually happens when moving in the sea ● Interesting title – wordplay
Weaknesses	● Last line 'When the long trick's over' difficult to understand compared with rest of poem	● Read aloud, not so obvious it is a poem
Mood	● Makes reader feel excited about the prospect of going to the sea ● Seen also in the title 'Sea fever' ● Optimistic	● Makes reader think and work out what 'lifting up horizontal and flapping limbs fishwise' means
Appeal to the reader	● Easy to read ● Easy rhyme – appears to have a melody as though it could be the lyrics of a song ● Something that lots of people would also like to do ● It is easy to get into your head	● Appeals because it has happened to everyone who has tried to move in the sea

(Exemplar material)

Modelling written comparison

Write this on the board ...	... while you are saying this
INTRODUCTION	*Use information from first two sections of planning frame – type and subject. First planning section shows a difference – blank verse/quatrain. Second shows a similarity – poet remembering times at sea.*
At first glance	*Interesting start to the sentence.*
these poems <u>seem</u>	*Present tense (examples underlined).*
to be quite different:	*Use semi-colons to separate the clauses stating why the poems are different.*
one is blank verse; the other is a quatrain with a very strong rhythm. *Yet*	*Contrast connective (examples italicised).*
<u>paying</u> closer attention,	*Complex sentence.*
the reader <u>realises</u> they are both about memories of the sea.	*Follow up with details of subject of each poem.*
The narrator of John Masefield's 'Sea Fever' really <u>wants</u> to go down to the sea once more and <u>lists</u> the things he expects to see again, *whereas* the narrator of Joseph Johnson's 'Disevolving' <u>is</u> <u>remembering</u> what it was like moving in the sea.	*Adding the title and name of poet clarifies the the subject of the comparison.*
MAIN BODY OF THE COMPARISON	*Main body includes strengths, weaknesses and mood. One way of approaching this section is to write about all three features in one poem and then the other (as below). Alternatively, write about the strengths of each poem, then the weaknesses, then the mood.*
The title 'Disevolving' <u>uses</u> wordplay and is one of the poem's strengths, as is the way it is written.	*Follow up with reasons.*
It really <u>makes</u> the readers ask themselves what <u>does</u> the poet mean, 'Lifting up horizontal and flapping limbs fishwise'?	*It is not always necessary in a comparison to explain the meaning.*
In contrast, 'Sea Fever' <u>is</u> easier to understand, apart from the last line 'when the long trick's over.' It <u>has</u> an optimistic mood and <u>gives</u> a feeling of excitement which is helped by its strong rhythm.	*Reinforce the importance of referring to specific lines in the text.*
CONCLUSION	*Use this section to sum up appeal of poems to reader. Opinions given (examples in bold), but in formal style – not 'I think'.*
Both of the poems **will appeal** to the reader because	*Give the reason why.*
they are talking about things which many people have experienced for themselves.	*Start with a similarity, then contrast with a difference in the following sentence.*
However, due to the strong rhythm of 'Sea Fever', it <u>is likely</u> that this is one readers will remember. The repetition of the line 'I must go down to the sea(s) again' makes it like the lyrics of a song, which will help readers to keep it in their heads for a long time.	*Gives further reasons why 'Sea Fever' is so memorable.*

Connectives of comparison and contrast

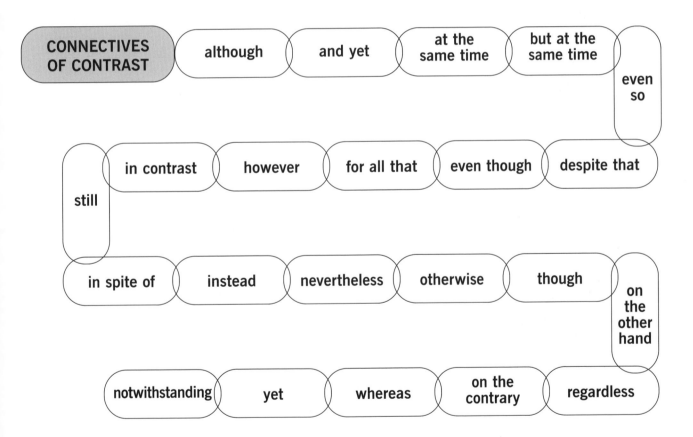

(**Pupil copymaster**)

Morwenstow

Where do you come from, sea,
To the sharp Cornish shore,
Leaping up to the raven's crag?
    From Labrador.

Do you grow tired, sea?
Are you weary ever
When the storms burst over your head?
    Never.

Are you hard as a diamond, sea,
As iron, as oak?
Are you stronger than flint or steel?
    And the lightning stroke.

Ten thousand years and more, sea,
You have gobbled your fill,
Swallowing stone and slate!
    I am hungry still.

When will you rest, sea?
    When the moon and sun
    Ride only on fields of salt water
    And the land is gone.

Charles Causley,
from Jack and the Treacle Eater

Classworks Literacy Year 6 © Paula Ross, Nelson Thornes Ltd 2003

(Exemplar analysis)

Example of analysis of *Morwenstow*

A direct question. First line finishes with the word 'sea'.

'Crag' = mass of rock projecting from a steep cliff.

More details about question.

Short answer from sea written in italics.

A direct question. First line finishes with the word 'sea'.

Second direct question that links to the previous one.

Short answer from sea in italics.

Second direct question linked to the previous one.

Short answer from sea in italics.

A statement about the sea. First line finishes with the word 'sea'.

More detail to accompany statement.

Short comment from the sea about statement.

A direct question.

Three-line answer from sea – rhyming pattern is weaker.

Rhyme pattern: alternate lines.

Use of words with similar meaning.

MORWENSTOW

Where do you come from, sea,
To the sharp Cornish shore,
Leaping up to the raven's crag?
From Labrador.

Do you grow tired, sea?
Are you weary ever
When the storms burst over your head?
Never.

Are you hard as a diamond, sea,
As iron, as oak?
Are you stronger than flint or steel?
And the lightning stroke.

Ten thousand years and more, sea,
You have gobbled your fill,
Swallowing stone and slate!
I am hungry still.

When will you rest, sea?
*When the moon and sun
Ride only on fields of salt water
And the land is gone.*

*Charles Causley,
from* Jack and the Treacle Eater

(Pupil copymaster)

How the Sea

"How the sea does shout,"
Says Danny Grout.
"Sounds very vexed.
What does it say?"
  Feed me a wreck,
  Said Sam-on-the-Shore.

"How the sea cries,"
Says Jimmy Wise.
"Early and late.
What does it say?"
  Send me some freight,
  Said Sam-on-the-Shore.

"How the sea moans,"
Says Johnnie Stones
Growing pale then paler.
"What does it say?"
  Send me a sailor,
  Said Sam-on-the-Shore.

"Shall we sail today?"
Says Dan, says Jim,
Also John.
  Don't fancy a cold swim.
  Homeward we go, boys.
  Put kettle on,
  Said Sam-on-the-Shore.

Charles Causley,
from The Young Man of Cury and Other Poems

(Exemplar material)

Checklists for poetry on a theme

Example of a checklist for analysing a poem for meaning

- Read through once and decide what the poem is about

- Read through again to find evidence to support your ideas

- Check each verse, using the following to decipher tricky parts:
  - context
  - knowledge of word roots
  - a dictionary (if available)

- Label verses/sections with a key word to sum them up

Example of a checklist of possible language features

- Use rhymes within the line or at the end

- Use full or half rhymes

- Use rhythm

- Use patterns including repetitions

- Use simile, metaphor and personification

- Use alliteration

- Use onomatopoeia

- Use assonance

- Use idioms

- Use unusual phrase or sentence structures

- Can choose your own punctuation (does not have to fit general rules)

Example of a checklist for comparing poems

- State the titles of the poems and the poets

- Identify similarities and differences between the poems

- Include details about the type and subject of the poems

- Include strengths and weaknesses of the poems

- Write opinions in a formal way (rather than 'I think …')

- Use technical vocabulary associated with poetry, for example, 'metaphor'

- State who the poem would appeal to and why

- Use connectives of contrast and comparison

(**Marking ladder**)

This unit covers a variety of objectives, from analysing meanings, to criticism, to writing own poems. You may want to use a marking ladder for any or all of these areas. It will be important to modify the ladder accordingly. An example has been included for writing a comparison of poems on the same theme.

Name: _____

Pupil	Objective	Teacher
	I clearly stated which poems are being compared.	
	I identified similarities and differences between the poems.	
	I included details about: • the form of the poems • the subject of the poems • their strengths • their weaknesses.	
	I presented opinions in the third person.	
	I included technical vocabulary associated with poetry, e.g. 'metaphor'.	
	I stated who the poem would appeal to and why.	
	I used at least three examples of connectives of contrast and comparison.	
	What could I do to improve my work next time?	

Phonics, Spelling and Vocabulary

I recommend that wherever possible the following word-level activities are made competitive, for example four teams working collaboratively, teams nominating a delegate each time to write the answer on the board, against the clock.

Spelling strategies

Mind map

- Build a mind map of words stemming from, for example, 'chrono-.

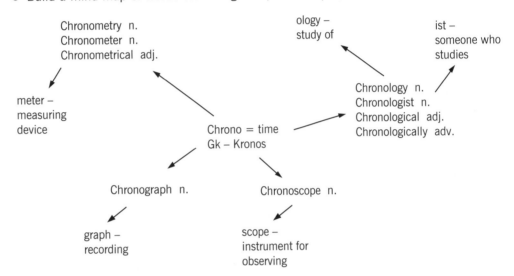

Mind maps can be built from any root word.

Incorrect spellings

- Write 20 words on the board, 12 of which are spelt incorrectly. The children identify the mistakes and state how they know, based on spelling rules and other knowledge. For example: 'intrest' – unstressed vowel missing; 'makeing' – remove 'e' when adding 'ing'.

Word chains

- Write a four-letter word, for example 'post', on the board. Child 1 changes one letter, spells the new word 'pose' and, if correct, this is added to the chain and the next child repeats the activity to form 'hose'. This can be extended to five-letter words.

Word matrices

- Generate words from roots, prefixes and suffixes. For example:

en		e
	velop	
		ed
		ing
		er

re	de		able	
un			ability	
under			ment	al

Word factory

- Generate lists of words from each morpheme of a particular word.

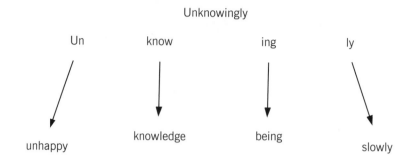

Add a suffix

- Write a list of suffixes on the board, for example, '-age', '-less-', '-or', '-ness', '-ful'. Call out a word, for example, 'help', 'sail', 'instruct', 'beauty'. The children select a suffix which is appropriate for the word and spell it correctly on whiteboards.

Add a prefix

- Write a list of prefixes on the board, for example, 'un-', 'dis-', 'im-', 're-', 'mis'-. Call out a word, for example, 'agree', 'possible', 'connect', 'lead', 'happy'. The children select a prefix which is appropriate for the word and spell it correctly on whiteboards.

Dictionary race

- Give a dictionary to each child or pair of children. Challenge the children to:
  - find identified words
  - find the word listed after a specified word
  - find the last word on the page/the word at the top of the column where 'dice' can be found
  - identify the word class(es) of specified words
  - find a noun, for example 'flame', and identify other linked words and their classes, for example 'flames', 'flamed', 'flaming', – verb.
  - find a word, identify its root and find other words stemming from the root and identify how the meanings are linked, for example, 'dormitory' – room providing sleeping quarters for several people; 'dormobile' – a vehicle where people can sleep; 'dormant' – asleep; 'dormouse' – a small rodent, with a reputation of spending much time asleep, from French *dormer* = to sleep.

Flashcards for a problem homophones

- Select homophonic words which present difficulties for children, for example, 'there', 'their', 'they're'. On a strip of card, write a word at each end and on the reverse of the card.

their	there

they're

Call out sentences including the word 'there', 'their' or 'they're'. Each time one of the words is spoken, the children show the correct version.

- On another occasion ask the children to invent their own sentences with 'there', 'their' or 'they're'. Individual children come to front of the class, say their sentence and check which 'there', 'their' or 'they're' the other children are showing. They then explain to peers who have made an error why their choice is inappropriate.

Spelling conventions and rules

Mnemonics

- Select words which many children often misspell. Help the children to find ways of remembering them, for example, 'interested' = 'inter'/'rest'/'ted' (**Ted** had a **rest** in the **inter**val).

  Ask the pairs to choose one word and, in two minutes, come up with a spelling strategy to remember it. This could be a mnemonic ('library' = Learning In Books Really Annoys Rude Youngsters), a word within a word ('Look for the *story* in history'), a play on the 'shy' unstressed vowel ('There's always an 'i' in business').

Mnemonics

- 'Show me' cards can be used in a whole class activity to consolidate identification by asking the children to write on whiteboards and hold up the 'shy' letter (unstressed vowel) in a word. Reinforce by having the whole group sound out the word with emphasis on the unstressed vowel.

I pack my ...

- Select a prefix, for example, 'bi-'. The first child says, 'I pack my bag and in it I put a bicycle', then the second child says, 'And it is spelt B I C Y C L E'. The third child then adds an item with the same prefix: 'I pack my bag and in it I put a bicycle and biceps', and the fourth child adds: 'It is spelt B I C E P S'.

Vocabulary extension

Origins and definitions

- Brainstorm the origins and definitions of particular names or words as appropriate for the unit. For example, for a journalism unit, brainstorm local and national newspaper names. ***Newspaper are about communicating; how do their names reflect this? Use a dictionary to find definitions and the origins of the names.***

Is it a?

- Read examples of metaphors and similes. The children use whiteboards to identify whether each one is a metaphor or a simile. For example:
  - 'The baby was like an octopus, grabbing at all the tins in the supermarket.'
  - 'No one invites Harold to parties because he's a wet blanket.'
  - 'The bar of soap was a slippery eel during the dog's bath.'
  - 'Ted was as nervous as a cat with a long tail in a room full of rocking chairs.'

Collections: similes

- Select an adjective, for example, 'dry', 'brittle', 'loud', 'vibrant', 'lonely'. Every one in the class writes their own simile for the adjective. For example: as loud as
  - *'an echo in an empty room'*
  - *'a siren at the crack of dawn'*
  - *'a toddler's scream'*
  - *'a teenager's stereo after school'.*

Homophones

- ***How many homophones can you include in the same sentence?*** For example: 'the bald man bawled at the boy when he kicked the ball through his window'. Try these: 'air', 'heir'; 'bare', 'bear'; 'knead', 'need'; 'right', 'write'; 'know', 'no'.

Word play – puns

- 'Our geography teacher says that her globe means the **world** to her.'
  'A dog not only has a fur coat but also **pants**.'
  Have a go: Think of words or phrases that you know that have more than one meaning. Find a word or words that sound similar to others to begin with. For example: 'in Seine' ('insane'); 'Taiwan' ('tie one').

Word-search of synonyms

- Collect as many synonyms as possible for 'nice', then make them into a word-search puzzle for someone else to try.

Onomatopoeia

- Onomatopoeia is the imitation of natural sounds in word form. For example: 'Bong!', 'Hiss!', 'Buzz!' In groups of three to four, the children brainstorm for three minutes. They list all the onomatopoeic words they can think of. They then swap lists between groups. The other group should write a person's name, a place or a thing that first comes to their mind when they hear the word.

Oxymorons

- Oxymorons are combinations of contradictory words, for example, 'pretty ugly', 'almost exactly', 'hard cushion'. Ask the children to invent their own.

Word work linked to text-level work

Find a name

- Ask the children to look through some reading books and make a list of names. They then decide what kind of narrative the name would fit. Repeat the activity with setting, weather and so on.

Build a character

- Pick a name and ask the children to draw the character and surround it with possible characteristics.

Collections: formal language

- From a collection of same genre texts, extract and classify words that, for example, are used in formal language. Ask the children to draw a up a glossary explaining what is meant by each word or phrases and provide a quotation using it in context.

Starters incorporating vocabulary extension with sentence-level work

Now say that again

- Challenge the children to describe brushing their hair without using the words 'hair' or 'brush'. For example, 'grooming your long, shiny tresses'. Similarly ask them to describe eating a piece of birthday cake without saying 'birthday' or 'cake', watching television without saying 'watch', 'television', 'TV' or 'look', and so on.

Making sentences

- Ask the children to provide a list of possibilities to improve the preciseness of sentences. For example, verbs such as 'achieve', 'act', 'afflict', 'allow', 'alternate', 'analyse', 'announce', 'answer', 'appeal', 'apply', 'argue', 'assemble', 'assess', 'assist', 'assume', 'avoid'. Write two nouns on the board, for example, 'the pensioner', 'the collie'. The children have to write sentences using the two nouns and selecting a verb.

Replacements

- From given sentences in the Making sentences activity (above) ask the children to replace the verb, the subject or object.

Substitution

- To stop the children always referring to characters in their writing by the same terms, ask them to substitute a noun phrase for the proper name. Examples: 'my grandfather', 'Grandpa, this hero of the 1930s', 'Old Blue Eyes', 'Mr Endurance' or 'Superman with a Walking Cane'.

Marking ladder

Name: _____

Pupil	Objective	Teacher
	What could I do to improve my work next time?	